PERSPECTIVE AND COMPOSITION

PARALLEL PERSPECTIVE
ANGULAR PERSPECTIVE
PICTORIAL PERSPECTIVE
PICTORIAL COMPOSITION

by

E. L. KOLLER, A. B., A. M.

*Director of Art Schools, International
Correspondence Schools; Member of
the American Federation of Arts.*

22

Published by

INTERNATIONAL TEXTBOOK COMPANY

SCRANTON, PENNSYLVANIA

INTERNATIONAL TEXTBOOK PRESS
Scranton, Pa.   91528

PREFACE

This volume is one of a series devoted to the training of those with Art aptitude for the field of illustration and design. It is not to be considered as a separate treatise, as would be in a cyclopedia, on the theory of perspective and composition, but as a necessary part of a systematic training in art for practical purposes.

Therefore, while one might work out perspective diagrams without a preliminary training in pictorial art, one should not attempt to prepare pictorial perspectives, or pictorial compositions, without some previous training in still-life and figure drawing, and in the handling of various artistic mediums and techniques. Such work is treated in other volumes of this series, the study of which will greatly benefit the reader of this present volume.

While a thorough training is given in the principles and practices of perspective drawing as a preparation for picture making, the diagrams and sketches are not mechanical or burdensome. They are so presented as to be applied readily to pictorial composition work. The concluding material in the volume, devoted to pictorial composition, gives a clear and thorough training in the laws of composition, and the methods of securing good pictorial compositions with one, two, three, or more, figures in the grouping.

It must not be forgotten that the mere reading of a book on any technical art subject cannot be expected to take the place of the actual training and practice secured by making the perspective drawings and compositions suggested. The one who reads this book, therefore, is advised to do the work specified in order to get this training. While comments from capable instructors constitute the ideal way of acquiring drawing and art ability, one can help one's self to a high degree by preparing the designated drawings and inspecting and commenting on one's own work.

E. L. KOLLER

CONTENTS

NOTE.—This book is made up of separate parts, or sections, as indicated by their titles, and the page numbers of each usually begin with 1. In this list of contents the titles of the parts are given in the order in which they appear in the book, and under each title is a full synopsis of the subjects treated.

PARALLEL PERSPECTIVE

ANGULAR PERSPECTIVE

PICTORIAL PERSPECTIVE

PICTORIAL COMPOSITION

PARALLEL PERSPECTIVE

A Pictorial Illustration in Which Parallel Perspective
is Used

PARALLEL PERSPECTIVE

Serial 1727 ——————— Edition 1

INTRODUCTION

PURPOSE

1. Need of Perspective in Pictorial Work.—Skill in drawing and rendering objects, figures, etc., though the drawing may show taste, cleverness, and originality, is not sufficient for the production of good pictures. Unless the principles of perspective are understood and applied, the foundation draftsmanship of a picture will be poor.

In a picture, which usually consists of a group of objects or figures, each object, or figure, must not only be properly drawn and foreshortened, but it must bear the proper relation of apparent size to all the others. The apparent size of each object, or figure, in a drawing depends on the actual position of the object with relation to the observer's eye; the size is therefore determined by applying the principles of foreshortening.

The application of the principles of foreshortening to the drawing of groups of objects, figures, houses, details of landscape, etc., is known as **perspective.** While it is possible to speak of a single foreshortened object being in perspective, the term perspective will here be confined to groups, and the term foreshortening will be used when single objects are being considered.

2. Pictorial Distinguished From Mechanical Perspective.—While it is necessary to become familiar with all the main principles of scientific perspective (as used in mechanical and architectural perspective drawings) in order to learn pictorial perspective, yet the process is not mechanically laborious. Although it is required to study and prepare certain charts and diagrams to learn the principles of locating certain points, lines, and planes, these are not minutely scaled mechanical or architectural diagrams, and therefore will present no difficulty to the art student.

However, some students may think that, because perspective is a more or less exact science, it is out of place in a study of artistic subjects; others, through a desire to reach quickly the more advanced portions of the Course, may desire to postpone or omit the study of this subject. Owing to its great importance, however, for artistic work cannot be done without an accurate groundwork, no student will be permitted to omit or postpone this subject unless he can submit drawings to show that he has had a complete training in perspective drawing elsewhere.

CLASSES OF PERSPECTIVE

3. Parallel Perspective.—Scenes may be viewed in various ways and from different positions, thus causing the angles at which they are viewed to differ. For instance, a house may be viewed from directly in front, so that the observer is looking right at the vertical center line of the front of the house, and sees only the front elevation of it and neither of the ends. In this case the front foundation line, upper and lower edges of front windows, etc. are horizontal lines.

The frontispiece, facing page 1, is a graphic example of a scene drawn in parallel perspective, with landscape accessories freehand. When a scene is viewed in this manner it is said to be in **parallel perspective** because many of the lines in the object are parallel to the face plane of the observer, and therefore parallel to one another.

4. Angular Perspective.—If the observer now walks to the right or to the left of his original position, he will then be looking at one corner of the house, and will see two sides of the house; that is, the front and one end. In this case all upright lines are vertical, but the foundation lines on the front and the side and the upper and lower edges of the windows seem to extend backwards from the observer's eye at different angles, and toward certain common points.   An object so viewed is said to be in **angular perspective.**

Under the head of angular perspective is usually considered **oblique perspective.**   In this case the observer, when viewing the house or other object concentrates his attention upon the sloping surfaces, such as roofs, gables, etc., and notices that they do not retreat toward some point or points on the horizon, but toward points above or below the horizon, whence the name oblique.

There is also to be considered the perspective of curves, circles, and other odd shapes, which, for convenience and for reasons that will be brought out later, are classed under angular perspective.

5.   Pictorial Perspective.—When an object or a group of objects, including such accessories as trees, clouds, landscape accessories, human figures, etc., is seen, or when such a scene is sketched or gotten up as a composition to serve as an illustration, it is termed **pictorial perspective.**   Pictorial perspective is not an isolated class of perspective, but depends on and includes parallel perspective and angular perspective; and unless these two preliminary classes of perspective are first mastered it will not be possible to sketch or compose illustrative work in accordance with the principles of pictorial perspective.

6.   Method of Treating Perspective.—The purpose of training the illustrator in perspective is that he may use correct perspective in his pictorial work.   Inasmuch as, to do this, he must first be trained in the principles of parallel, angular, and pictorial perspective, it will be necessary to use three Sections for the proper presentation of the principles and practice of perspective.   This present Section, therefore, will be devoted to parallel perspective; the following Section, to angular perspective; and a third Section, to pictorial perspective.

PRINCIPLES OF PARALLEL PERSPECTIVE

FACTORS IN A PERSPECTIVE VIEW

7. Points, Lines, and Planes.—An example of a simple parallel perspective view would be that taken down the

FIG. 1

middle of a street, showing the retreating lines of car tracks, sidewalks, verandas and window sills of buildings, etc., and the apparent decrease in size as the buildings get farther from the eye, such as is seen through the window pane in Fig. 1. However, to determine just how such a scene is drawn there must first be learned the factors that go to make up such a view and, later, the drawing to be made from it.

In every perspective view there are certain definite factors; that is, points, lines, planes, etc., that determine the sizes and proportions of the parts in a perspective drawing. The most important of these are the *station point, line of sight, visual angle* or *scope of vision, picture plane, horizon line, ground line, vanishing lines, vanishing points,* and *measuring points.*

8. Station Point.—That point from which the entire view is seen, namely, the eye of the observer, is called the **station point.** Theoretically, a group of objects or a scene is viewed from a single point, not from two; therefore, the station point is taken to be the eye of the observer, which on the average is about $5\frac{1}{2}$ feet above the ground. In Fig. 1 the station point (as also in every other case where the observer is viewing a scene), is the eye of the observer.

9. Line of Sight.—When one looks directly at an object, a group of objects, or a scene, there is usually one part of the scene that he sees most clearly first; therefore the visual ray of light that comes from this clearest part to his eye (or, conversely, the line that may be considered as going from his eye to that part) is called the **line of sight.** In the case shown in Fig. 1 the line of sight is from the man's eye to the point in the distance where tracks, sidewalks, building lines, etc. appear to meet. It must be understood that there are also other visual lines coming from every point in the scene to the observer's eye; these will be referred to when the picture plane is discussed.

10. Visual Angle, or Scope of Vision.—The human eye is so constructed that it is capable of seeing only what is included in an angle of about 60°, and so the field of view is limited to about 30° on each side of the line of sight. When so limited, the field of view is termed the **visual angle, or scope of vision.**

The truth of this statement is easily found by making a demonstration similar to that shown in Fig. 1, where is shown a long straight stretch of street. To the observer looking out through the window not only do the retreating lines appear to meet at a distant point, but the street seems narrower and the houses smaller at that distant point than in the foreground of the scene. One's own knowledge and experience tell him that the street is just as wide and the houses are just as large at that distant point as they are in the foreground of the scene; and yet they really appear of smaller size.

17. Ratio of Apparent Decrease in Dimensions. That the apparent size of an object depends on its distance from the observer may be easily demonstrated by experimenting with objects of the same size. For example, if two lead

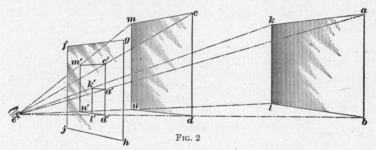

FIG. 2

pencils of exactly the same size are held, vertically, the same distance from the eye they will appear to be of equal size. But if one pencil is held steady while the other is slowly moved farther from the eye, the pencil that is moved will apparently decrease in size and become smaller than the other.

That this apparent decrease in size is regular and can be estimated with exactness may be proved by holding one pencil in the right hand 12 inches from the eye and the other pencil in the left hand 24 inches from the eye, or just twice the distance. The pencil in the left hand will then seem to be just one-half the size of the pencil in the right hand. If the pencil in the left hand is placed 48 inches from the eye, or four times as far away as the pencil in the right hand, it will appear to be only one-fourth as large as the pencil in the right hand.

18. In Fig. 2 is shown a graphic illustration of this principle, as it shows two rectangles of the same shape and size, such as two books, sheets of cardboard, etc., placed vertically before the eye *e*. One of these rectangles *m c d n* is placed 12 inches from the eye *e* and the other *k a b l* 24 inches, or twice the distance. By extending the light rays from the corners of the rectangles to the eye, and thus projecting points upon an assumed picture plane (in this case transparent plane *f, g, h, j*), and then connecting these points, the images of the two rectangles may be obtained. A comparison of these images will then show that the image *k' a' d' l'* of the farther rectangle is only one-half as high and one-half as wide as the image *m' c' d' n'* of the nearer rectangle.

Thus it is seen that this apparent decrease or increase in size is always based on a certain ratio, no matter what is the size of each object or how great or little the distance. The apparent height or width of the object varies inversely as its distance from the eye; that is, as the distance increases the apparent size decreases, and as the distance decreases the apparent size increases.

19. Ratio of Apparent Decrease in Area.—The diagram in Fig. 2 also shows that the apparent areas of the surfaces vary in a different proportion to the height and width. As shown by the images *k' a' d' l'*, and *m' c' d' n'*, the area of the rectangle *k a b l* is apparently only one-fourth the area of the rectangle *m c d n*.

Thus the apparent decrease or increase in area of objects can always be based on a certain ratio, no matter what is the size of the objects or their distance from the eye. The apparent area of the object varies inversely as the square of the distance (that is, the distance multiplied by itself) of the object from the eye; that is, if one object is twice as far from the eye as another its apparent area will be inversely two times twice as great; that is, four times the area taken inversely, in other words, one-fourth the area. If four times the distance away it would appear $4 \times 4 = 16$ taken inversely; in other words, one-sixteenth the area.

MAKING DRAWINGS IN PARALLEL PERSPECTIVE

VIEWING THE SCENE

20. **Main Characteristics of Parallel Perspective.**
An example of a scene in parallel perspective is shown in Fig. 3, which is a view down the middle of a long straight stretch of single-track railway, with the telegraph poles and wires,

Fig. 3

fences, and other landscape accessories. This figure, however, must not be considered as a picture but as the actual view seen by a person standing midway between the rails of the track. He will then observe that all vertical lines, and all horizontal lines that are actually parallel with the picture plane, retain their normal positions and angles; none of them vanish. But all receding horizontal lines, that is, those extending backwards away from the eye, vanish at a common point on the horizon. For this reason, parallel perspective is sometimes referred to as **one-point perspective.**

The scene is thus being viewed for the purpose of making therefrom a perspective drawing.

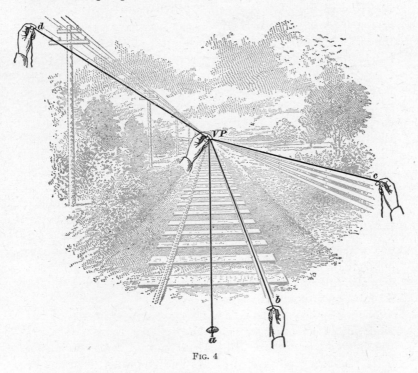

FIG. 4

21. Locating Vanishing Point When Partly Revealed. As the making of an accurate perspective drawing depends in great measure on the location of the vanishing point, the first step is to seek for and locate this vanishing point. In a scene like that shown in Fig. 3 this is not difficult. It is quite apparent that the vanishing point is located where the retreating lines of the rails, fence boards, telegraph wires, etc., appear to meet.

However, there is considerable difference between actually seeing the very evident position of the vanishing point in a picture of a scene and finding the location of the vanishing point in an actual scene.

To find the vanishing point in a scene like that shown in Fig. 3, hold one end of a string (about 2 or 3 feet long and weighted at one end) level with the eye and at arm's length in front of the body. If the hand holding the string (when viewed with but one eye open) is at the point where the rails of the track appear to meet, the loosely hanging string will take the position of the line VPa, Fig. 4. If this weighted end is now moved a little to the right by means of the right hand, the string will coincide and cover the right-hand rail of the track, as shown by the line VPb. If this end is moved farther to the right and upwards, the string will soon coincide with and cover the top edge of the top board of the fence, as shown by the line VPc. Similarly, the vanishing lines of the telegraph wires may be found by holding the string in the position of the line VPd.

22. If in any of these tests the string does not exactly coincide with all the lines mentioned, the left hand (shown as VP in Fig. 4) should be moved slightly to the left, to the right, up, or down. When finally the point is established that will allow the string to coincide, in successive tests, with each retreating line as tested, then the vanishing point VP in the actual scene will be determined.

The student is expected to make several experiments of this kind; for in no other way can he obtain a thorough understanding of perspective. But in all cases these experiments must be made from actual scenes and not with diagrams or pictures.

23. Locating the Hidden Vanishing Point.—The experiments just given should also be made in those cases in which the vanishing point is hidden, as when looking down the center of a straight street, a long hallway, or a room. In the case of a room, one end of the string should be held directly in front of the eye and coinciding with the vertical center line of the end wall. If the other end is then moved to the right, the string can be made to coincide with and cover the line made by the right-hand wall with the floor. If it is moved above the horizon on the right, it can be made to cover the line where the ceiling meets the right-hand wall; or, if it is a little lower, the line of the tops of the windows. Similarly, the string may be made to cover the lines on the left-hand side of the room. After all these tests have been made, it will be found that the vanishing point, in all cases where it is not at first apparent, is in reality on the vertical center line of the end wall and on a level with the eye.

STAGES OF PROCEDURE

NOTE.—As he studies the descriptions of Figs. 5, 6, 7, 8, 9, and 10, the student is expected to make similar drawings. These drawings, however, are not to be sent to the Schools for examination; they are to be made simply for practice and to make the descriptions given more easily understood.

24. To make a perspective drawing, it is necessary to have an approximately correct idea of the following points:

1. The size of the object, or objects, in plan view, in front view, and in side view. The approximate size is sufficient.

2. The distance of the observer from the objects and his definite relation to them.

3. The position of the assumed picture plane with relation to the observer and the objects.

4. The relative size to which the drawing is to be made; in other words, the scale of the drawing.

When these facts are known, *scaled drawings* (that is, drawings in which inches, or fractions thereof, represent feet in the actual scene), should be made of the top, front, and side views of the objects. Afterwards these drawings should be combined so as to produce the perspective drawing. When the principles and methods of making perspective drawings are thoroughly understood, though, this process will be greatly simplified.

25. Aids in Making Perspective Drawings.—While the purpose here is to teach freehand pictorial work, there are certain devices that enable a person to make the drawings more easily. Among these are the *triangles* and *scale rule*.

The **45° triangle** has two sides of equal length but the third side is longer; its two equal angles are 45° each and the third is 90°. This triangle will be found very useful in the laying out of the lines and angles in parallel and 45° angular perspective.

The **60° triangle** has all sides of different lengths; its angles are 30°, 60°, and 90°. This triangle is used when angular perspective drawings of 60° and 30° are being made.

26. A scale rule is somewhat like an ordinary 1-foot rule though the divisions along its edges are different. One set of marks may show the important divisions $\frac{1}{4}$ inch apart; as each division then represents 1 foot in the actual scene or object the scale is known as a scale of $\frac{1}{4}$ in. = 1 ft. If it were desired to measure inches, each $\frac{1}{4}$ inch would be divided into twelve equal parts, each of which would represent 1 inch. The average illustrator will not use such small dimensions. Another set of marks make the important divisions $\frac{1}{2}$ inch apart; this scale is known as a scale of $\frac{1}{2}$ in. = 1 ft. An ordinary 1-foot rule may, however, be used for the scale rule in most cases.

When the vanishing or construction lines are longer than the scale rule or longest edges of the triangles, an edge of a sheet of drawing paper or other straightedge may be used.

27. Determining Sizes of Objects and Position of Observer, Picture Plane, Etc.—It is not necessary to get the exact measurement of the object to be drawn; it is sufficient to determine the approximate size. In most cases this is easily done. For instance, a man's height is usually taken as $5\frac{3}{4}$ feet; therefore the height of a house, tree, etc. by which a man is standing may be easily computed. The sizes of ground areas, house plans, etc., also, may be easily determined. A simple frame residence is usually 35 feet wide by 40 feet long, whereas a more pretentious brick or stone house may be 45 feet wide by 60 feet long. Building lots may be $22\frac{1}{2}$, 45, or 90 feet wide and of proportionate depth. The distances between objects and their positions in relation to one another can be estimated in the same way, by comparing them with lengths or distances that are already known.

28. It is especially important that the distance from the eye of the observer to the nearest object be estimated with approximate accuracy, for this determines the position of the picture plane, which in turn influences the size of the perspective drawing. This distance can be pretty accurately judged, in the manner just described for the size of objects, by comparison with a man's height or by using one's knowledge of actual dimensions of areas or distances. Thus, if the sketch is to show a man standing on a corner of a 60-foot street, an artist sketching from the other side of the street knows that the man is about 60 feet away; or, if sketched from the middle of the street, that he is 30 feet away.

The most convenient position in which to arbitrarily place the picture plane is in contact with the near face of the nearest prominent object in the scene. In this way actual scaled measurements can be laid out on the picture plane.

29. Determining Proper Scale of Drawing.—The size of the sheet of drawing paper is usually limited, say to 10 in. $\times$ 15 in., or perhaps 15 in. $\times$ 20 in. Therefore, it is impossible to make a full-size drawing of a man $5\frac{1}{2}$ or 6 feet tall, standing 7 or 8 feet away from the objects to be drawn. A proper *scale* for making the drawing must, as a result, be decided on; that is, one must know how small or large he may make the drawing in order to keep it within the confines of the sheet and that each part of the drawing may bear the same relative proportion to every other part of the drawing that the corresponding feature in the actual scene bears to all the other features in the scene.

30. Preliminary Drawing of Top View.—In order that the method of making a perspective drawing may be fully understood, an illustrative example will be given. It will be assumed that three boxes, 2 feet in each dimension, are placed in a line extending away from the observer, the nearest box standing 7 feet from him. A very convenient scale is

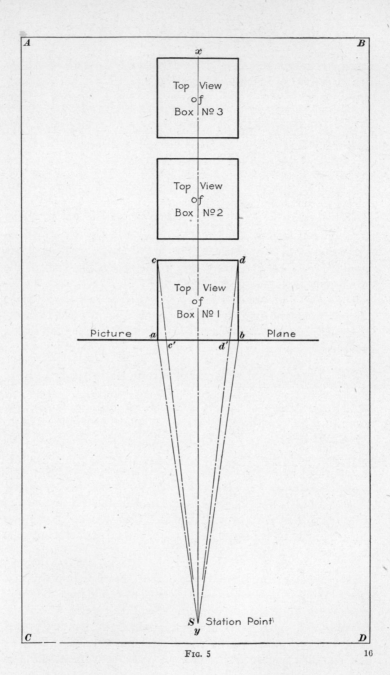

Fig. 5

1 in. = 1 ft.   If this is adopted in the present instance. each box will be two times 1 inch or 2 inches square and the distance of the observer from the picture plane will be seven times 1 inch or 7 inches.   The other dimensions and distances will be in the same proportion.   The student should make his drawings on paper 10 in. × 15 in. and use the exact scaled measurements given; his drawings will then be twice the size of the text illustrations, which are reproductions of the original drawing and are only one-half of the desired size.

31.   In drawing the top view, which is shown in rectangle $A B C D$, Fig 5, the first step is to lay out the three boxes, which are the stationary features of the scene.   As the boxes are 2 feet wide, 2 feet high, and 2 feet deep, their tops are 2 feet by 2 feet.   Using a scale of 1 in. = 1 ft., the size of each box top would be two times 1 inch, or 2 inches.   As the boxes are placed 6 inches apart, this distance in the drawing will be six-twelfths or one-half of 1 inch, or $\frac{1}{2}$ inch.   Thus the boxes can be laid out to scale on the vertical center line $x\, y$.

For convenience, the picture plane may be of indefinite extent and placed in contact with the front side of the nearest box.   As it is vertical, when viewed from above this plane will appear, as shown in Fig. 5, as a heavy black line, because only the top edge will be seen.

The observer is 7 feet away from the nearest face of box *No. 1,* and on the central line $x\, y$ of seeing, because he is looking directly at the front box in parallel perspective.   But 7 feet in the actual scene, when scaled, is only seven times 1 inch, or 7 inches on the drawing.   Therefore S, the position of the eye of the observer, is laid off, on the line $x\, y$, 7 inches from the picture plane, as shown in Fig. 5.

32.   There are now located the positions of the objects, the picture plane, and the observer (or the station point), so that it simply remains to project lines of light rays from the various corners of the boxes toward the station point S.   These will determine the lateral dimensions of the image on the picture plane; in other words, the lateral dimensions of the perspective view.   The length $a\, b$ of the front edge is already

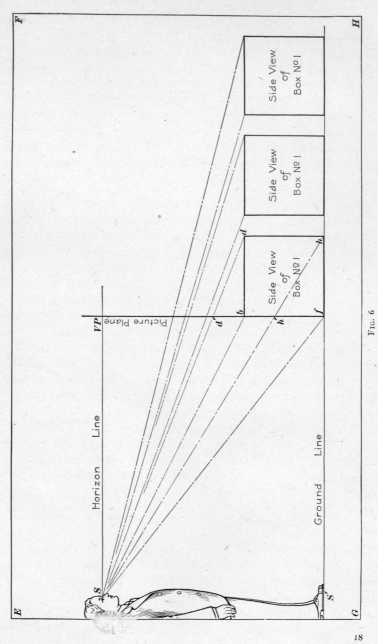

Fig. 6

18

perspective height of the rear vertical face of the box. The perspective heights of boxes *No. 2* and *No. 3* are found in the same manner.

These perspective vertical dimensions, and the method of finding them, must be kept well in mind so that they may be combined with the perspective lateral dimensions, as found in Fig. 5, the combinations and intersections of projection lines from both forming the perspective view, as will be described later.

35. Drawing the Perspective View.—The perspective view, shown in Fig. 7, is the image that the observer, whose eye is at *S*, Figs. 6 and 7, sees upon the picture plane. It is made by combining, by projected parallel lines, the lateral projected measurements secured from the scaled plan and the vertical perspective measurements secured from the scaled side view. This process, which is shown in Fig. 8, is as follows:

Paste two 15″×20″ sheets of paper together on the 20-inch edge. Then, lay out in the upper left-hand portion of the sheet rectangle *A B C D* and its contents on a scale of 1 in. =1 ft.; this rectangle will be an exact duplicate of rectangle *A B C D*, Fig. 5. Then lay out, at the lower right-hand part of the sheet, rectangle *E F G H* and its contents on a scale of 1 in. =1 ft.; this rectangle will be an exact duplicate of rectangle *E F G H*, Fig. 6. Care must be taken, however, to make *S* of rectangle *E F G H*, Fig. 6, fit over, and coincide exactly with *S* of rectangle *A B C D*, Fig. 5, and after the fitting process has been accomplished, to mark the point *V P* as shown in Fig. 8. In this way the lower right-hand portion of rectangle *A B C D* will be slightly overlapped by the upper left-hand portion of rectangle *E F G H*, as shown in Fig. 8.

36. If the contents of both rectangles have been fully drawn to scale, the lines can now be projected to form the perspective elevation, as follows: From points on the picture plane in the top view (*a*) parallel lines are projected vertically downwards; and from points on the picture plane in the side view (*b*) parallel lines are projected horizontally toward the left. Where corresponding projected lines cut each other will be located other points, which, when connected by straight lines will form the image seen on the picture plane by the observer looking at it squarely from in front.   To find the perspective of the front face of box *No. 1*, parallel vertical lines should be projected downwards from points *a* and *b* in the top view (*a*) to meet horizontal parallel lines projected over from points *b* and *f* in side view (*b*), thus locating points *a, b, e,* and *f*.   These, when connected by straight lines, form the front face of box *No. 1* in the new rectangle *I J K L*, which will be the perspective view (*c*). Similarly, to find the perspective of the rear face of box *No. 1*, parallel vertical lines should be projected downwards from points *c'* and *d'* in top view (*a*) to meet horizontal parallel lines projected over from points *d'* and *h'* (found by projecting lines from *d* and *h* to *V P*), in side view (*b*), thus locating points *c, d, g,* and *h,* in perspective view (*c*).   These, when connected by straight lines, form the rear face of the box *No. 1* in perspective in new rectangle *I J K L*.   Now, if points *a* and *c, b* and *d, e* and *g,* and *f* and *h* are connected, the entire outline of the box in perspective will be completed.   Of course, because the box is opaque, edges *c g, d h, g h, g e,* and *h f* will not be seen. It should be noticed that if edges *a c, b d, e g,* and *f h* are extended backwards away from the eye, they will meet at the vanishing point *V P*, and on the horizon.   The outline perspectives of boxes *No. 2* and *No. 3* are found in exactly the same way; but, to avoid confusion, the dotted projection lines and reference letters for locating boxes *No. 2* and *No. 3* are not shown in Fig. 8.

37.   The order in which every perspective drawing is made may be briefly stated as follows: First, the top view (or plan) at the top of the sheet is laid out; then the side view at the lower right-hand portion of sheet; next lines projected toward *S*, or *V P* as shown in the final drawing, (in both cases) from the points until they cut the picture plane; from these points so located on the picture plane parallel lines (dropped vertically from the top view, and projected horizontally to the left from the side view) are projected so that corresponding projection lines cut each other at right angles; when these points are

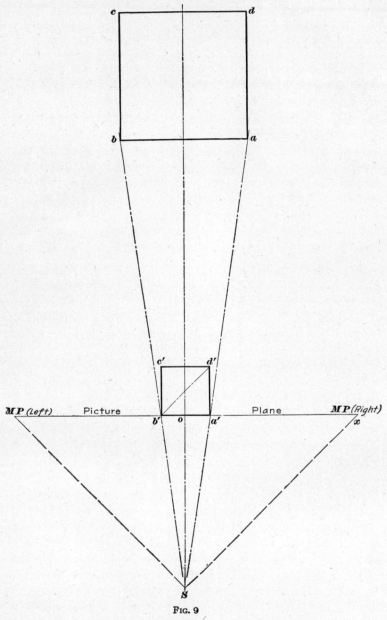

FIG. 9

connected up by straight lines, the desired perspective drawing in outline is secured.

38. Use of Measuring Points.—The principle on which every parallel perspective drawing is made is that shown in Fig. 8, but the top view and the side view are not always laid out and lines projected therefrom. Ordinarily, only the horizon line and ground line are laid out. The perspective view is then constructed by laying off vertical and horizontal measurements directly on the picture plane and projecting them back toward the vanishing point, and finding measurements on retreating horizontal lines by establishing measuring points, $M P$ (*Right*) and $M P$ (*Left*), on the horizon line. Actual measurements are then projected from the ground line toward these measuring points until they cut the proper retreating line.

39. The system by which the right and left measuring points are obtained is illustrated in Fig. 9, where the large square $c\,d\,b\,a$ may be considered the actual top view, full size, of a distant cubic object that is being viewed. At $c'\,d'\,b'\,a'$ is the apparent size of the image of the top view as viewed by the eye when this top view is reduced to the scale to be employed in the drawing, which is 1 inch (in the drawing) corresponding to 1 foot (in the actual object). Therefore, $c'\,d'\,b'\,a'$ is 2 inches square, and it is against the face of this 2-inch square that the picture plane is placed. It is known that the retreating sides of the top view of the box vanish toward $V P$ on the horizon, which point in Fig. 9 is marked o, but the problem is to find where they stop vanishing, in other words, what their length in perspective will be. To do this, the familiar principle of the right-angle triangle is used. In Fig. 9, the plan of the box is a square $c'\,d'\,b'\,a'$. If the diagonal $b'\,d'$ is drawn, a right-angle triangle $b'\,d'\,a'$ results, in which side the front edge $b'\,a'$ of the base of the box is the same length as the right-hand retreating edge $a'\,d'$ of the base of the box. The vanishing point of the diagonal $b'\,d'$ on the base of the box is where the line of sight of the observer, when looking toward the right parallel to the diagonal line, cuts the picture plane on the horizon line. Transferred to the

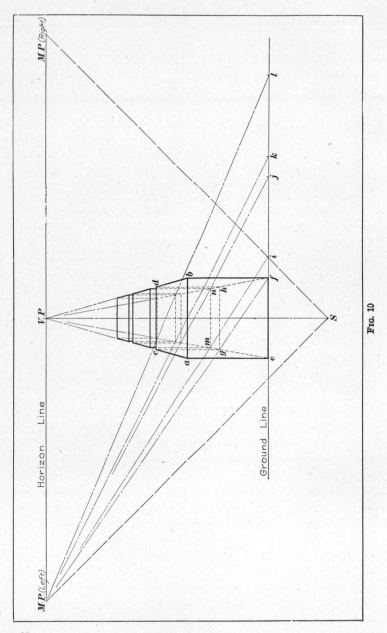

Fig. 10

perspective diagram or drawing, it is simply necessary to draw a line *S x* through *S* parallel to the diagonal *b′ d′* of the square so as to cut the picture plane.   This will occur at *M P* (*Right*). *M P* (*Left*) is located in a similar manner to the left of *o*.   It is seen that *M P* (*Right*) and *M P* (*Left*) are therefore exactly the same distance from central point *o* as is *S*.   In other words, the measuring points in parallel perspective are placed on the horizon, to the left and right, respectively, of the center of vision, a distance equal to the distance of the observer from the picture plane.

40. Simplified Method of Making Drawing.—By employing the system of measuring points just described a simplified method of laying out the perspective drawing may be used, as shown in Fig. 10.   First is laid out the horizon line at the upper part of the sheet of paper, and $5\frac{1}{2}$ inches below it (representing $5\frac{1}{2}$ actual feet) is laid out the ground line. Then, as the station point *S* is in this case 7 feet from the picture plane, it is laid off seven times the foot unit, or 7 inches, below the picture plane line, as shown at *S*, Fig. 10.   This must always be accepted as an arbitrary fact; namely, that *S* is placed a scaled distance below the horizon equal to the actual distance of the observer from the picture plane.

41.   Next, the full size 2-inch square *a b f e* should be laid out, the lower edge resting on the ground line as shown, because (as it is in contact with the picture plane) there is no fore-shortening or perspective needed in this front face.   Next, lines should be vanished back from corners *a, b, f,* and *e,* to central vanishing point *V P* on the horizon, thus determining the positions (but not extent) of the tops and bottoms of the three boxes.   There is thus located the direction in which the tops, bottoms, and sides vanish, but not the limits of these vanishing sides.   In other words, there remains to be found the place at which they stop vanishing, that is, the perspective depths of the boxes.   The measuring points *M P* (*Right*) and *M P* (*Left*) will enable one to secure definite measurements for perspective depths.   It was shown in Fig. 9 that if line *b′ d′* is vanished back at 45°, it will locate the rear right-hand corner of the box; in the same manner line $a'\,c'$ will locate the rear left-hand corner of the box. Applying this principle to Fig. 10, if a line is vanished back from f toward $M\,P$ (*Left*), (which is really the vanishing point for all 45° lines to the left, but which in the case of parallel perspective serves as a measuring point), this line will cut vanishing line $e\,V\,P$ at g, locating the rear left-hand corner of the base of the box in perspective. Similarly, a line projected back from point e toward $M\,P$ (*Right*) will cut vanishing line $f\,V\,P$ at h, locating the rear right-hand corner of the base of the box in perspective.

42. The principle is that, to lay off any perspective depth on a line vanishing to $V\,P$ in parallel perspective, one need simply lay off the actual measurement on the ground line (which may now be considered the measuring line) and project it backward toward $M\,P$ (*Left*) or $M\,P$ (*Right*), as the case may be, until it cuts the line vanishing to $V\,P$. Thus, to get perspective depth of 2 inches, the 2 inches is laid off at $e\,f$ on the measuring line, projected back to $M\,P$ (*Left*) so as to become $e\,g$ on the vanishing line $e\,V\,P$. Similarly, to find, in perspective, how far apart will be the rear of box *No. 1* and the face of box *No. 2*, it is simply necessary to lay off the actual scaled distance (6 inches actually, or $\frac{1}{2}$ inch to scale) at $f\,i$, and project it back to $M\,P$ (*Left*) until it becomes $g\,m$ on vanishing line $e\,V\,P$. In a similar manner the 2-inch length $i\,j$ on the measuring line projected back gives the perspective depth of box *No. 2*. Box *No. 3* and its distance from box *No. 2* are found in the same way.

Only the positions of the bases of the three boxes have so far been found; but it simply remains to erect vertical lines $e\,a$, $f\,b$, $g\,c$, $h\,d$, etc., to cut the upper vanishing lines $a\,V\,P$ and $b\,V\,P$, thus determining the top corners of the boxes. Straight lines connecting the points so located will complete the outline perspective of the three boxes, as shown in Fig. 10.

EXTERIOR VIEW IN PARALLEL PERSPECTIVE

NOTE.—As he studies the description of Fig. 11, the student is expected to make a similar drawing. This drawing, however, is not to be sent to the Schools for examination; it is to be made simply for practice and to make the description given more easily understood.

43. Rows of Tents in Parallel Perspective.—There are some views in nature that are seen only in parallel perspective; for example, a view down a closely built-up street, through a tunnel, between rows of tents, etc. All such views have one vanishing point, which is at or near the center of the picture.

In Figs. 11, 12, and 13 is shown the method of drawing a parallel perspective of two rows of tents, three in each row. In (*a*) is shown the top view of the tents and the observer *S*. In (*b*) is shown the side view; that is, the side that is toward the observer of one of the tents; and in (*c*), the front view of one of the tents. It is not necessary that there should be definite measurements in feet and inches for these tents when the top, side, and front views are so accurately drawn, but for convenience dimensions are here given.

Each tent is 9 feet wide by 9 feet deep and 6 feet from its neighbor. It is 8 feet high to the peak and the vertical side, where the flap starts, is 3 feet high. The rows of tents are 10 feet apart, in other words, the street between the tents is 10 feet wide.

A convenient scale to use when making the drawing is $\frac{1}{4}$ inch on the drawing represents 1 actual foot in the view. If desired, though, the scale $\frac{1}{2}$ in. = 1 ft., may be used. In Fig. 11, the scale of $\frac{1}{4}$ in. = 1 ft. was used for the original drawing; the illustration, of course, is on a reduced size, on account of the limitations of the size of the page.

44. Locating Perspective Widths.—The method of procedure when laying out the drawing is exactly the same as described for the boxes in Fig. 8. First, in Fig. 11, the horizon line is drawn, then $5\frac{1}{2}$ feet to scale (that is, $5\frac{1}{2}$ times the 1-foot unit, $\frac{1}{4}$ inch, or $1\frac{3}{8}$ inches) below the horizon line the ground line is drawn. The observer is 22 feet away from the nearest tent; therefore, S is laid off **22** times $\frac{1}{4}$ inch, or $5\frac{1}{2}$ inches, below the horizon line. The measuring points $M P$ (*Left*) and $M P$ (*Right*) are laid off the same distance from $V P$. Point $V P$ is on the horizontal line directly above S, in the perspective view (*d*), because it is on the central line of vision. Points $M P$ (*Right*) and $M P$ (*Left*) are the same distance from $V P$ as S is from the picture plane; that is, from the horizon line in the illustration. Thus, in perspective view (*d*) $M P$ (*Left*) is $5\frac{1}{2}$ inches to the left of $V P$, and $M P$ (*Right*) is $5\frac{1}{2}$ inches to the right of $V P$. Lines $S M P$ (*Left*) and $S M P$ (*Right*) are then drawn, not for any definite structural part of the diagram but to preserve graphically the proper relations between the station point and the measuring points.

45. The simplest method of drawing in perspective an object that has irregular sides is to consider it as being laid out or included in a rectilinear solid. First, then, in Fig. 11, lay off on the ground line (which is also the measuring line), in perspective view (*d*), the dimensions of $c\,d$, $d\,x$, and $x\,y$, taken from top view (*a*); that is, 9 feet, 10 feet, and 9 feet, respectively. The 10-foot dimension $d\,x$ should be centered on the line of sight $S\,V\,P$ in the perspective view (*d*). Point d_1 will then be $1\frac{1}{4}$ inches to the left, and point x_1 $1\frac{1}{4}$ inches to the right, of the center line $S\,V\,P$, in the perspective view (*d*). Distance $c_1\,d_1$, or the base of the front tent of the left-hand row, will be $2\frac{1}{4}$ inches. Verticals $c_1\,a_2$ and $d_1\,b_2$ should then be erected each 8 feet high; that is, to scale, actually 2 inches high in the drawing. This will give the front side of the $9'\times9'\times8'$ rectilinear enclosing solid in which the tent is to be drawn.

46. To find the width of the front of the tent in perspective, that is, its perspective depth, the same plan of using the measuring point is employed as was used in the case of the boxes, Fig. 9. The points d, e, f, g, h, and i from the top view (*a*), (that is, $d\,e=2\frac{1}{4}$ inches, $e\,f=1\frac{1}{2}$ inches, $f\,g=2\frac{1}{4}$ inches, $g\,h=1\frac{1}{2}$ inches, $h\,i=2\frac{1}{4}$ inches), are laid out on the ground line in the perspective view (*d*), starting at point d_1 and extending toward the right. From these points, e_1, f_1, g_1, h_1, and i_1, in

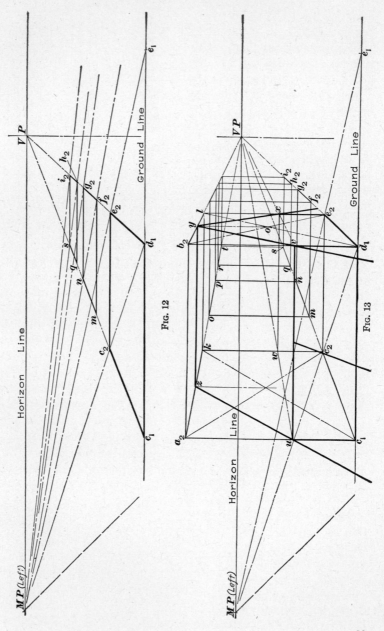

FIG. 12

FIG. 13

Fig. 12 lines are projected back to $M P$ (*Left*) and where they cut the vanishing line of the fronts of the tents $d_1 V P$ will mark points e_2, f_2, g_2, h_2, and i_2. These points determine the location of the fronts of the tents and their distances apart in perspective. This is shown in Fig. 11, but is shown more clearly in Fig. 12 which is drawn on a somewhat larger scale, in which all the intersecting points are marked. For instance, e_1 projected back to $M P$ (*Left*) determines e_2, and thus $d_1 e_2$ is the front of the nearest tent. Line $e_2 c_2$ can then be drawn parallel to the picture plane, and where it cuts the vanishing line $c_1 V P$ of the backs of the tents will determine the rear side of the tent. Thus points c_2, e_2, d_1, c_1 are located as the base of the front tent in perspective, as shown in Figs. 11 and 12.

47. It simply remains to erect verticals $c_1 a_2, d_1 b_2$, each 8 feet high (to scale), and $c_2 k$ and $e_2 l$ to meet retreating lines $a_2 V P$ and $b_2 V P$, connect points k and l, and the perspective view of the rectilinear solid in which the tent is to be drawn is secured as in Figs. 11 and 13. To determine the points where the sloping sides start away from the vertical sides, measure $c_1 u$ and $d_1 v$, Fig. 13, in perspective view (*d*), 3 feet. Project these points backwards to $V P$ until the vanishing lines cut verticals $c_2 k$ and $e_2 l$ at w and x, respectively, in Fig. 13; then lines $u v$ and $w x$ are the lines from which the sloping sides start.

48. Locating Perspective Heights.—As the ridge line of the tent will be the center line of the top $k l b_2 a_2$, Figs. 11 and 13, it is necessary to find the center points, in perspective, of lines $b_2 l$ and $a_2 k$. These, of course, could be measured upon and projected from the ground line, but a simpler method is based on the fact that the diagonals of a parallelogram intersect at the center of the parallelogram, and a line drawn through their point of intersection parallel with two of the sides will bisect the other two sides of the parallelogram and also the parallelogram itself. For example, in Fig. 13, the front view of the tent and enclosing rectangle or parallelogram, the diagonals $b_2 e_2$ and $l d_1$ intersect at o the center of the parallelogram, and a vertical line $o y$ drawn through their point of

INTERIOR VIEW IN PARALLEL PERSPECTIVE

NOTE.—As he studies the description of Fig. 14, the student is expected to make a similar drawing. This drawing, however, is not to be sent to the Schools for examination; it is to be made simply for practice and to make the description given more easily understood.

51. Ordinarily, interior views are arranged in angular perspective to give a more artistic effect, but there are occasions, as when drawing a hallway, room, etc., when parallel perspective must be used. Except in the case of a hall or long room, when making a perspective drawing of an interior, the observer is supposed to be standing outside of the room. It is also supposed that a large sheet of glass takes the place of the side nearest the observer; this glass is the picture plane. As the observer must be so placed that the widest part of his image does not exceed the 60° angle of vision, the station point S should be placed, from the picture plane, about $1\frac{1}{2}$ times the greatest width of the room.

52. To show the method of making an interior view in parallel perspective, this view will be drawn of a small business office that is 10 feet long, 10 feet wide, and has the ceiling 10 feet high; in other words, a hollow cube. To make this drawing, it is necessary to lay out, to scale, at the top of the sheet, a plan view of the room, as is shown in Fig. 14 (a). On this view should be marked the doors at the left-hand side and rear and the two windows and desk on the right-hand side. To obtain a 60° angle, the station point S, in this case, should be placed about $11\frac{1}{2}$ or 12 feet (to scale) from the picture plane.

At the lower left-hand portion of the sheet lay out the left-hand side view with one door, as is shown in (b). At the lower right-hand portion, lay out the right-hand side view with two windows and a desk, as is shown in (c). In (d), the perspective view is shown constructed. The horizon line throughout these three views, (b), (c), and (d), must be kept on the same level.

53. Locating Perspective Measurements on Left-Hand and Rear Walls.—To locate the perspective measurements on the left and rear walls, draw the horizon line in view (d) through S of view (a) and then, $5\frac{1}{2}$ feet (to scale) below it, draw the ground line. Upon this ground line, and centered on the central line of vision $S V P$, lay out $c_1 d_1$ 10 feet long (to scale) as the base line of the front of the room. Then erect verticals $c_1 a$ and $d_1 b$, each 10 feet high (to scale), and draw a horizontal line $a b$, which completes the open front of the room $a b d_1 c_1$.

To locate the position and size of the rear wall of the room, project a line back from point d_1 on the ground line toward $M P$ (*Left*); where this line cuts the retreating line $c_1 V P$ will mark off a point e 10 feet back (in perspective) from the front of the room c_1. Locate the point f in a similar manner. Then erect verticals $e e_1$ and $f f_1$, until they cut retreating lines from a to $V P$ and from b to $V P$, respectively, and thus determine the position and size of the rear end of the room $e_1 f_1 f e$. This completes the room interior, $a b d_1 c_1 e_1 f_1 f e$.

54. To locate the width of the door in the center of the rear wall, lay off upon a strip of paper the dimension points e, g, and h found at the upper part of plan view (a). Then transfer these actual dimensions to the space within the distance $c_1 d_1$ on the ground line in the perspective view (d). The actual dimensions in the top view (a) are $e g = 3\frac{1}{2}$ feet, $g h = 3$ feet, and $h f = 3\frac{1}{2}$ feet, which may be transferred to $c_1 d_1$ by scaled measurements, but this is not necessary if the strip of paper is used. From points g_1 and h_1, vanish the lines back to $V P$ until they cut the floor line of rear wall at points g_2 and h_2. Verticals erected from points g_2 and h_2 will then determine the width of the door in the rear wall.

To find its height, the actual height of the door must be projected from the left-hand side view (b) over to the right until it cuts the vertical $c_1 a$ (which serves as a vertical measuring line because it is on the picture plane) at point i. From there it is vanished back toward $V P$ until it cuts the left-hand vertical edge of the rear wall at j. From this point a horizontal line is drawn to the right, across the rear wall until it cuts the verticals erected from points g_2 and h_2 at k and l. Therefore, k, l, $h_2 g_2$ is the position and shape of the rear door.

55. To locate the width of the door on the left-hand side of the room, the same principle is employed as was used to locate the points of the tents and their distances apart, in Figs. 11 and 13. The actual dimensions are secured from the left-hand side wall, in view (a), and are laid off on the edge of a slip of paper and then transferred to the ground line in the perspective view (d), starting from point c_1 and measuring toward the right. As the arrangement of the left-hand wall is the same as that of the rear wall, the same points g_1 and h_1 are used from which to project lines backwards as were used to locate the door in the rear wall. From these points, lines are projected backwards to $M\,P$ $(Left)$ which cut vanishing line $c_1\,V\,P$ in g_3 and h_3. Then, from these points are erected verticals that determine the location and perspective width of the doorway of the left-hand side wall. This doorway is exactly the same height as the rear doorway, and therefore the projection and vanishing lines used to determine the height of the latter will also determine the height of the former. So, where retreating line $i\,j$ cuts the verticals erected from points g_3 and h_3, points g_4 and h_4 are located. Thus, $g_4\,h_4\,h_3\,g_3$ forms the position and contour of the left-hand side doorway.

56. Locating Perspective Measurements on Right-Hand Wall.—The locations and sizes of the windows and desk on the right-hand wall are determined in the same way. First the points $d, q, m, n, r, o, p,$ and f, from top view (a) [or the actual dimensions, if desired, $d\,m = 1\frac{1}{2}$ feet; $m\,n = 2\frac{1}{2}$ feet; $n\,o = 2$ feet; $o\,p = 2\frac{1}{2}$ feet; $p\,f = 1\frac{1}{2}$ feet; and $q\,r$ (the desk) $= 3$ feet] should be laid off on the edge of a strip of paper as previously described and transferred to line $d_1\,c_1$ in perspective view (d), starting at d_1 and measuring toward the left. Reading from right to left, the points then become $d_1, q_1, m_1, n_1, r_1, o_1,$ and p_1. From these points lines are now vanished back toward $M\,P$ $(Right)$ and where these vanishing lines cut the retreating base line of the right-hand wall $d_1\,f$ (vanishing toward $V P$), points will be shown as located in the diagram. Verticals erected at all these points, except q_2 and r_2, will determine the positions and widths of the windows on the right-hand wall. Verticals erected at q_2 and r_2 will determine the perspective length of the desk.

57. To find the heights of the windows and of the desk, their actual heights must be projected over to the left from right-hand side view (*c*) so as to cut vertical $d_1 b$, which will occur in points *s* for the top line of the windows, point *t* for the bottom line of the windows, and point *u* for the top of the desk. A line from *s* vanished back to *V P* will cut the erected

FIG. 15

window verticals, thus establishing the top lines of the windows. The bottom lines of the windows are located by vanishing a line back from point *t* to *V P* and cutting the proper verticals at points it is not necessary to mark. A line vanished back from *u* will determine the top rear line of the desk, line $r_2 q_2$ being the bottom rear line of the desk.

To find how far the desk extends into the room, lay off its actual depth $v d$ on line $d_1 c_1$ of view (*d*) and project back to parallel horizontal lines drawn to the left from points r_2 and q_2, thus determining points w and x. The shape x, r_2, q_2, w is now the bottom of the desk in perspective. To draw the perspective top of the desk the same method is followed as in the case of the boxes, namely, verticals are erected at w and x, parallel horizontal lines are run over from the top rear edge, and the points of intersection thus establish the top of the

Fig. 16

desk in perspective, and finally the shape of the entire desk is thus formed.

58. Other furniture in the room, pictures on the wall, etc., may be determined in a similar manner. Such accurate plotting, however, is not always necessary, for when once the inside contours of the walls, floor, ceiling, doors, and windows have been determined, the other accessories may be placed by eye measurement freehand, proportioning them properly to objects already determined. The important point is that the eye level of all standing figures in the picture must be the same and must conform to the eye level of the observer, which is $5\frac{1}{2}$ feet (to scale) above the floor of the room.

59. Converting the Diagram Into a Picture.—This explanation of the principles of perspective so far has required the use of diagrams with retreating lines, vanishing points, measuring points, dimensions, etc. Perspective is an exact science, and unless its principles are thoroughly learned they cannot be successfully applied to pictorial work. It is expected that each point has been carefully mastered, for otherwise these principles cannot be successfully applied to pictorial work. The method of converting the diagram into a picture is shown by means of Figs. 15 and 16; they also show the necessity of these diagrams. Fig. 15 shows, to an enlarged scale, the perspective view shown in Fig. 14 (d); but all vanishing and projection lines and lettered points have been omitted.

60. The diagram of the perspective view (d) in Fig. 14 is of necessity quite small in scale so as to be contained on the page, although the drawing of it will be considerably larger. In Fig. 15 is shown the perspective of the room [that is, portion $a\,b\,d_1\,c_1$ of perspective view (d), Fig. 14] enlarged so as to show the details more clearly, the vanishing lines, projection lines, and lettered points being omitted. This will now represent about all that need be drawn according to the rules of accurate perspective, and also includes certain details of furnishings, and a figure seated at the desk that had been sketched in freehand simply in outline. It will serve as the framework upon which may be worked up the pictorial rendering as shown in Fig. 16. The doors and windows, which were accurately laid out in Fig. 14, have been detailed more fully on an enlarged scale in Fig. 15, by sketching in the details, knobs, panels, etc. of the doors (open or closed), and the sashes, glass, shades, etc. on the windows; also pictures on walls, calendar, lighting fixtures, etc. have been drawn. The blocked-out form of the desk is accurately determined in the outline perspective in Fig. 14; therefore, it is easy to sketch in freehand in Fig. 15

and to render pictorially in Fig. 16, the panels, drawers, knobs, blotter, telephone, stationery, etc., on the desk, and the chair in front of it, and to put in properly the man seated at the desk. Fig. 16 shows the completed rendering evolved from the framework of the accurate perspective drawing in Fig 14.

In other words, only the skeleton lines of the main portions of a picture need be drawn according to the exact principles and rules of perspective; these then can be clothed with pictorial detail put in with all the freedom of freehand work and artistic rendering as may be desired. The final result will then be thoroughly artistic and natural because it has as its foundation an accurate perspective layout.

PERSPECTIVE DRAWING EXERCISES

GENERAL INFORMATION

61. Required Work in Parallel Perspective.—The only way by which it is possible to show that the principles of parallel perspective are thoroughly understood is by making pictures in which these principles are applied. There will, therefore, be required two exercises in the form of drawing plates. These exercises must be carefully worked out from the directions given. It will not do to make copies of the figures in the text, for some of the distances, dimensions, etc., specified in the Exercises following, have been purposely altered.

62. Preliminary Practice Work (Not To Be Sent In).—The system of doing some preliminary practice work, to get familiar with the principles of the subject, should be followed in this subject as in former ones. Therefore, before starting on Plate 1 the following preliminary drawings should be made, but are NOT to be submitted to the Schools. The only drawings to be sent in are for the regular plates, bearing definite numbers, and described later.

On a sheet of 15″×20″ paper arranged horizontally, make an outline pencil drawing in parallel perspective of the three boxes shown in Fig. 10. Each box is to stand on the ground and be 2 ft. × 2 ft. × 2 ft., and 6 inches from its neighbor. The observer S is to be 10 feet away from the nearest box. The scale of the drawing is to be 1 in. = 1 ft., which will make S in the drawing 10 actual inches below the horizon line; this line will be 20 inches long and placed about $2\frac{1}{2}$ inches below the top edge of the sheet of drawing paper. Points $M P$ (*Left*) and $M P$ (*Right*) will then be 20 inches apart; that is, at the extremities of the 20-inch horizon line. Draw all vanishing points, vanishing lines, and construction lines clearly and distinctly and allow them to remain; nothing should be erased. The outlines of the objects themselves should be emphasized. The proportions will differ slightly from those in Fig. 10.

63.   Character of the Drawing Plates.—As previously stated, there are to be two regular drawing plates submitted, and these—if done with the proper care—will, along with the training given by the preliminary practice work, give the student a thorough drill in parallel perspective.

Each plate will be 15 inches × 20 inches in size, the full size of the regular 15″×20″ sheet of white, cold-pressed drawing paper, and sent in as directed.

PLATE 1

64.   Exercise for Plate 1.—For the perspective exercise for Plate 1, on the sheet arranged horizontally make an outline drawing in parallel perspective of the two rows of tents shown in Fig. 11. Make the vertical and horizontal measurements of tents, street, etc., as shown in the top view (*a*) and side view (*b*). Place the observer S 40 feet away from the nearest tent and make scale of drawing $\frac{1}{4}$ in = 1 ft. This will make the horizon line 20 inches long and S will be placed in this case 10 inches below it. Measuring points $M P$ (*Left*) and $M P$ (*Right*) will then be 20 actual inches apart, and S 10 actual

inches below the horizon line.   Do not erase any lines after
drawing is made.   Proportions will differ slightly from Fig. 11.

65.   Final Work on Plate 1.—Letter or write the
title, Plate 1: Parallel Perspective, at the top of the sheet,
and at the lower left-hand corner, on the back, place class letters and number, name and address, and the date of completing
the plate.   Roll the plate, place in the mailing tube, and send
to the Schools for inspection; then proceed with Plate 2.

PLATE 2

66.   Preliminary Perspective Drawing for Plate 2.
For the perspective exercise of Plate 2, on the sheet arranged
horizontally, first make an outline pencil drawing in parallel
perspective of the room interior, after the method shown in
Fig. 14.   Select a suitable scale for the drawing, which may
be $\frac{1}{4}$ in. = 1 ft., or more, depending on the size of the sheet, with
$M\ P$ (*Left*) and $M\ P$ (*Right*) 20 inches apart.   It may be
necessary to use a $15'' \times 20''$ sheet, or even two $15'' \times 20''$ sheets
may be placed together, on two long edges.   The student must
judge for himself the scale of the drawing and the size of the
sheet required.   The result should be that the room interior will
be at least 4 inches square.

The completed drawing will resemble Fig. 15 in its method
of construction with the following change: The two windows
and desk, which in Fig. 14 appear on right-hand side, must be
placed at rear wall; and the door, which, in Fig. 14, is shown
in rear wall, must be placed in right-hand side wall.   The left-
hand side wall may be made as shown in Fig. 15.

67.   Rendering of the Perspective Drawing.—Using
as a basis the outline parallel perspective view of the interior
secured by making the parallel perspective, as described in the
preceding article, prepare a rendering over this perspective interior similar to the one shown in Fig. 16.   Note, however, that
the position of the desk (and man seated at it) and windows
has been changed as described in Art. **66.**

The rendering may be done in pen and ink (as shown in
Fig. 16), or in wash or water color, as preferred.

68. Final Work on Plate 2.—Letter or write the title, Plate 2: Parallel Perspective, at the top of the sheet, and at the lower left-hand corner, on the back, place class letters and number, name and address, and the date of completing the plate. Roll the plate, place in the mailing tube, and send to the Schools for inspection.

If any redrawn or rerendered work on the plates of this subject has been called for and has not yet been completed, it should be satisfactorily finished at this time. When all required work on the plates of this subject has been completed, the work of the next subject, in which angular perspective is taught, should be taken up at once.

ANGULAR PERSPECTIVE

An Example of the Application of Angular Perspective
Used in a Typical Illustration

ANGULAR PERSPECTIVE

Serial 1728-3

Edition 1

GENERAL PRINCIPLES

1. Characteristics of Angular Perspective.—Angular perspective differs from parallel perspective in the respect that in angular perspective the object or scene is not viewed from directly in front, but at an angle. For example, a man standing at one corner of a street intersection will see a part of each street and the most prominent object will be the building on the corner diagonally opposite the observer. The front and sides of this building, though, will appear to retreat from the eye of the observer at certain definite angles, in the same manner as did the sides of the foreshortened wooden cube when seen at an angle, when model drawing was studied.

As shown in Fig. 1, the angles at which an object or scene may be viewed vary greatly; but in all cases the picture plane is supposed to be at right angles to the line of sight. In this case, the boxes are shown in parallel perspective. But if they are viewed from any other position they are seen in angular perspective.

2. 45° Angular Perspective.—When the observer stands at S, Fig. 1, which is the station point, he views the boxes in parallel perspective. If he walks around toward the right on the heavy dotted curved line, to position S 45°, and then looks at the nearest box, he is viewing the box in angular perspective, which is called **45° perspective.** It is understood that the picture plane is swung around on corner b so as to be kept at right angles to the line of sight S 45° b. This shifting of the picture plane is always understood when the observer's position is shifted. The appearance of the boxes when so viewed, that is, in 45° perspective, will be as shown in Fig. 2.

3. 60° and 30° Angular Perspective.—Objects and scenes are not always viewed in such an arbitrary position

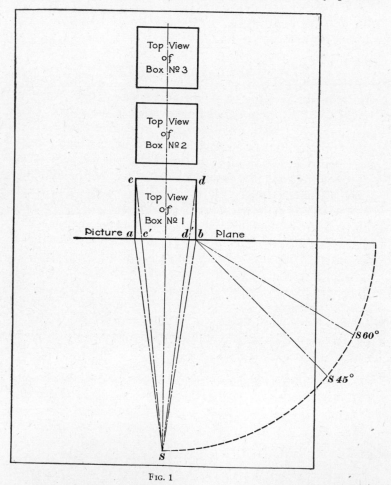

FIG. 1

as exactly at 45°. For example, the observer may be standing in such a position that he sees more of the right-hand side than of the left-hand side of the house, box, or whatever is being viewed; this means that the left-hand side is making a greater angle with the picture plane than is the right-hand side.

If, in Fig. 1, the observer continues to walk around to

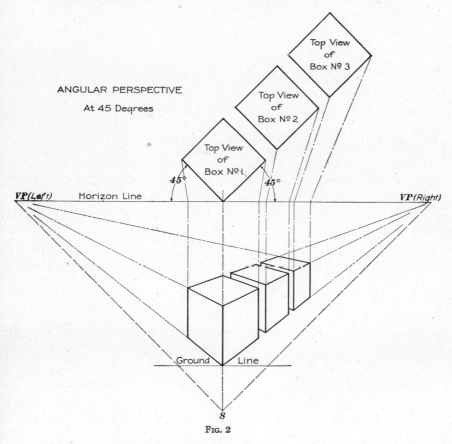

FIG. 2

position *S 60°*, and the picture plane is again shifted to be at right angles with the new line of sight, *S 60° b*, the left-hand side of the box makes an angle of 60°, and the right-hand side an angle of 30°, with the picture plane. When so viewed the box is said to be in **60° and 30° perspective.**

The appearance of the boxes in 60° and 30° perspective would
be as shown in Fig. 3.   It will be noted in Fig. 3 that the full
extent of the horizon line and vanishing lines running to *VP*
(*Right*) cannot be shown in the illustration, on account of the
lateral limits of the page.   It must be understood, however,
that all lines shown extending toward the right would meet
at *VP* (*Right*).

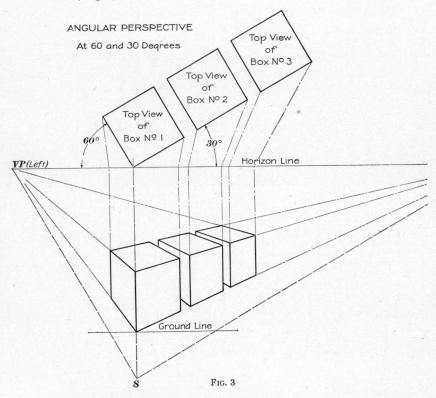

Fɪɢ. 3

If Fig. 2 and Fig. 3 are very carefully compared, point for
point, the distinction between 45° perspective and 60° and 30°
perspective will be clearly understood.   Such comparison must
actually be made by the student, so that these points may be
fully understood before he starts to make any drawings in
angular perspective.

view, lines should be dropped vertically from the picture plane of the top view to meet lines projected to the left from corresponding points on the picture plane of the side view. But in angular perspective this procedure is not necessary. All that is required is to draw the top view (a) of the boxes at an angle of 45° with the picture plane; locate the station point S at the usual place; project lines from the corners of the boxes toward S until they cut the picture plane, from which points drop parallel vertical lines into the perspective view (b) laid out as before. In the perspective view (b), draw the horizon line through point S of the top view (a), which point becomes o when it gets into the perspective view (b), then draw the ground line $5\frac{1}{2}$ feet (to scale) below the horizon line. Lay off the front vertical edge fb of the nearest box 2 feet (to scale) high and then draw vanishing lines bVP (Right), fVP (Right), bVP (Left), and fVP (Left). VP (Left) and VP (Right) are termed vanishing points, because they are the points to which the retreating lines vanish. In 45° perspective, as in parallel perspective, these points are the same distance from point o, in perspective view (b), as is the lower S. There are really not two S's, that is, station points; the two S's appear in perspective view (b) simply because it is overlapped by top view (a).

10. From the projected point d_1, in the top view (a), drop a vertical line so as to cut the vanishing line bVP (Right) at d, and continue it down to cut the vanishing line fVP (Right) at h. Line dh thus becomes the rear vertical edge of the right-hand side of the box. Similarly, project point a downwards from view (a) to locate rear vertical edge ae, in perspective view (b). If vanishing lines aVP (Right) and dVP (Left) are now drawn, they will cross and thus locate rear corner c, thus completing the entire outline shape of box No. 1 in 45° perspective; namely, $acdbhfe$. Boxes No. 2 and No. 3 may be drawn in a similar manner.

Although (to avoid confusion) not all the lines are shown extended entirely down toward S, they should be so extended when the student makes the drawing in order to be accurate.

DRAWING BY SIMPLIFIED METHOD

11. Use of Measuring Points.—The simplified method of making a drawing is as applicable to angular perspective as it is to parallel perspective. But the method of finding the measuring points is different. In parallel perspective, the measuring point on the right was found by locating on the horizon line the vanishing point of the 45° line, or the diagonal of the square. This was found by drawing a line through S parallel to the diagonal until it cut the picture plane on the horizon, at a point marked MP (*Right*). This then served as a measuring point toward which to project lines from actual measurements on the ground line. Point MP (*Left*) was found in a similar way.

12. In angular perspective, the points where these diagonals, in parallel perspective, vanish become the vanishing points $V P$. They are found by drawing through the station point lines parallel to the left and right sides of the square. As in parallel perspective, these points are located on the horizon line and, in 45° perspective, are as far from the center line $S o$ as the station point is from the picture plane.

13. The method of locating the two measuring points in angular perspective is an arbitrary one, and must be remembered by the student. The measuring points for all lines are on the horizon line as shown in Fig. 5. The measuring point for the lines vanishing to the right is as far to the left of VP (*Right*) as the distance VPS; the measuring point for the lines vanishing to the left is the distance $V P S$ to the right of $V P$ (*Left*). To locate the measuring points, therefore, it is simply necessary to mark the distance $V P S$ on a strip of paper and then lay this off to the right and left, respectively, of the vanishing points, or to swing around arcs from the two $V P$'s as centers, and with radius $V P S$ so as to cut horizon line. It must be remembered that $M P$ (*Right*), the measuring point for lines vanishing toward the right, is on the left of the center line and that $M P$ (*Left*), the measuring point for lines vanishing toward the left, is on the right of the center line.

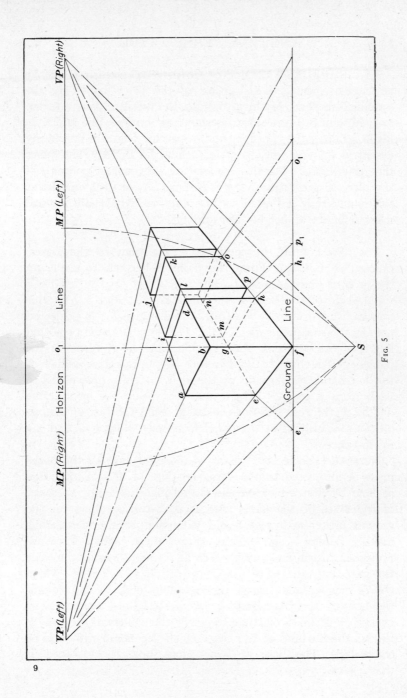

FIG. 5

9

16. The system of locating the tops of the boxes in perspective, and thus the entire boxes themselves, is the same as was used in parallel perspective. Verticals of indefinite extent are then erected at all the corners f, e, g, and h of the perspective plan of the nearest box. The nearest vertical fb is laid off, to scale, the actual height of the box, 2 feet, and lines are then vanished from b to $V P$ (*Right*) and to $V P$ (*Left*). Where these lines cut the verticals erected from points e and h will locate a and d, respectively. Lines vanished from a to $V P$ (*Right*) and from d to $V P$ (*Left*) will cross at c, which will be the rear corner of the top of the box. Thus the entire outline, $a\,c\,d\,b\,h\,f\,e$, of the box in perspective is formed. The perspective formation of the other two boxes is obtained in a similar manner.

17. Testing Accuracy by Projecting Lines.—The accuracy of the perspective drawing of the boxes in angular perspective can be checked up by drawing the top and side views, and then projecting lines over to the right and the left to meet vertical projected lines from above. Connecting the resulting points will result in an angular perspective drawing in outline, coinciding with the one just drawn.

EXTERIOR VIEW IN ANGULAR PERSPECTIVE

NOTE.—As he studies the description of Fig. 6, the student is expected to make a similar drawing. This drawing, however, is not to be sent to the Schools for examination; it is to be made simply for practice and to make the descriptions given more easily understood.

18. Rows of Tents in Angular Perspective.—To show the general principles governing an angular perspective drawing of an exterior view, the two rows of tents, previously drawn in parallel perspective, will be drawn. In this case, however, the tents are viewed when at an angle of 45° to the picture plane instead of parallel to it. Fig. 6 (*a*) shows the top view of the tents; (*b*) shows the side view of the tents toward the observer's left; (*c*) shows the front view of a tent. The front of each tent faces the street that runs between the two rows.

19. Locating Perspective Widths.—It is not necessary to explain point by point how the angular perspective drawing of the tents is laid out, for the procedure is exactly the same as in the case of the boxes shown in Fig. 5, except that there are two rows of tents. The scale of the drawing may be $\frac{1}{4}$ in. $=1$ ft., as used in the parallel perspective view (or $\frac{1}{2}$ in. $=1$ ft., if desired). After the top, side, and front views are laid out as shown, the horizon line and the ground line are laid off. Then the nearest corner d_2 of the plan of the nearest tent in view (a) is laid off on the ground line, at d_4, in perspective view (d), on the central line of sight $S\,o$. Then the plans of the six tents, three in each row, should be drawn in perspective, although to avoid confusion the plans of only the nearest two tents are shown.

20. Mark on a slip of paper, points c, d, c_2, and d_2 from top view (a), indicating the widths of the tents (each 9 feet, to scale), and the width of the street (10 feet, to scale). Then lay off these points, from the slip of paper or by scaled measurements, on the ground line in perspective view (d), measuring from d_4 toward the left. These points then become d_4, c_5, d_3, and c_3. Locate measuring points $M\,P$ $(Right)$ and $M\,P$ $(Left)$ by means of measurements on a slip of paper, or by swinging arcs around with a radius of $V\,P\,S$. From points c_5, d_3, and c_3, on the ground line, project lines toward $M\,P$ $(Left)$ until they cut the left vanishing line $d_4\,V\,P$ $(Left)$ (the near vanishing sides of the two front tents) in c_1, d_1, and c_4, which with d_4 will locate the four near corners on the left. From points c_1, d_1, c_4, and d_4 vanish lines back to $V\,P$ $(Right)$, to establish the lines of the fronts and backs of the rows of tents. Care must be taken here to note that the rows of tents are vanished to $V\,P$ $(Right)$, not to $M\,P$ $(Left)$.

21. To plot the *depths*, or the front or rear dimensions of the tents, and their distances apart, take actual (scaled) dimensions d_2, e_2, f_2, g_2, h_2, and i_2 from the top view (a), and transfer them to the ground line in perspective view (d) to the right of point d_4; this will establish points d_4, e_3, f_3, g_3, h_3, etc. From these points project lines back toward $M\,P$ $(Right)$, until they cut the right vanishing line $d_4 V P$ (*Right*), at e_4, f_4, g_4, h_4, etc.; this will locate the tent corners on the right. Lines vanished back from points d_4, e_4, f_4, g_4, h_4, etc. will cut the right vanishing lines from d_4, c_4, d_1, and c_1 to $V P$ (*Right*) at certain points which, when connected, will determine the plans of the entire six tents in perspective, the two front plans being shown in perspective view (*d*), Fig. 6.

22. Locating Perspective Heights.—After the plans have been drawn in perspective, the process of completing the drawing of the tents is exactly the same (in principle) as in the case of the tents drawn in parallel perspective. First, imaginary rectilinear solids (or boxes) to enclose the tents should be drawn by erecting perpendiculars from all four corners of each one of the six tents; these will cut the right and left vanishing lines retreating from point d_5 as a basis ($d_4 d_5$ being the 8-foot height of the tent), and from the top corners of the other imaginary solids containing the tents. The result of this will be six boxes in perspective, each one 9 feet wide by 9 feet long by 8 feet high. A tent can be constructed within each one of these boxes, by locating a point v 3 feet above d_4, and vanishing it backwards in all directions to the vertical sides of all six tents, thus determining the point or line from which the inclined tops or flaps will start. The ridge of each tent is found by drawing the center line of each top, using the principle of the diagonals of a parallelogram as previously described. When this has been done, the nearest tent will appear as shown in which the ridge line is drawn. By extending the slanting edges of the front and rear gables, the positions of the guy ropes are determined and the center one on each side is sketched in freehand.

contact with the wall. From these points lines are projected forwards, by using VP (*Right*) as the other end of the projection lines, and thus locating points on the verticals, erected from the four corners of the base of the desk. Thus points are secured which, when connected, will give the skeleton outline of the desk in perspective. It must be understood that this accurate method of locating a piece of furniture in a room is given merely to show the principle by which it is done. In pictorial sketching, or composition work, the position and size of the desk is sketched in by eye measurement in relation to the other details of the room.

ROOM INTERIOR WITH MEASURING PLANE AT REAR

28. Placing of Plane.—The method of drawing an angular perspective view that is shown in Fig. 8 is simpler and more convenient than that used so far. The scaled dimensions of the visible details of the room are laid off on a plane that is in contact with the rear corner, these dimensions then being projected forwards to the various vanishing lines and the verticals. This method, however, is purely diagrammatic, and is used only as a short cut; the student must never lose sight of the fact that, in an actual perspective view, the scene is always back of the picture plane and is projected forwards toward the observer, who is in front of the picture plane.

29. Locating Perspective Measurements.—In this method, the plan of the two adjacent walls is laid out as before. Then the full-scale dimensions are taken from the plan and laid out directly upon the ground line, which is at the base of the measuring plane at the rear corner of the room. The station point S, in top view (*a*), Fig. 8, is located a considerable distance away from the measuring plane, say twice as far away as the widest part of the room scene, which would be about 21 feet, to scale. Then, the horizon line and the ground line are laid off, as before, in perspective view (*d*), and, on the ground line, the lower distant corner of the room is located. A vertical ff_1, 10 feet high, to scale, represents the distant corner edge of the room. All vertical measurements are taken upon this, because it is the only part of the room that is in contact with the measuring plane.

In the perspective view (*d*) locate lower *S* about 21 feet, to scale, below the horizon line, and then *V P* (*Left*) will be 21 feet, to scale, to left of the center line *S f*; and *V P* (*Right*) will be 21 feet, to scale, to the right of *S f*. The top and bottom lines of the left wall $e_1 f_1$ and *e f* will vanish at *V P* (*Right*)

Fig. 9

and the top and bottom lines of the right-hand wall $j f_1$ and $d_1 f$ will vanish at *V P* (*Left*). The positions and widths of the left side of the room itself and of the rear door may now be laid off. The actual dimensions can be taken from top view (*a*) and transferred to the ground line in perspective view (*d*), thus becoming points e_2, g_1, h_1, and y_1 on the ground line to the left of *f*. Through these points, lines are then projected from *M P* (*Right*) until they cut the vanishing line *e f* at points e, g_2, h_2, and y_2. The side verticals $e\,e_1$ of the left side of the room and $g_2\,k$ and $h_2\,l$ of the door may now be erected.

Similarly, lines should be projected from $M\,P$ *(Left)* through points p_1, o_1, n_1, m_1, and d_2 on the ground line to the right of f until they cut the vanishing line $d_1\,f$ in points p_2, o_2, n_2, m_2, and d_1, at which points other verticals are erected, which represent the windows and desk, and the right side of the room. The heights of door, windows, and desk are found as before.

FIG. 10

CONVERTING THE PERSPECTIVE DIAGRAM INTO A PICTURE

30. It is only necessary to lay out the skeleton or framework of the scene in perspective. All the accessories may be put in freehand, thus giving an opportunity for using originality and artistic execution. The amount of accurate perspective drawing that is required in a given case is shown in Fig. 9; Fig. 10 shows this skeleton after it has been pictorially rendered. These companion illustrations show that the framework of

to avoid confusion it is also laid off at $c\,b$. To the left of the central point of vision a, points k, h_1, f_2, f_3, h, g, f, e_1, f_1, o_2, e, and d are laid off, from actual measurements from the plan. They are then projected forwards to vanishing line $a\,c_1$ and locate the positions and widths of the chimney fireplace, chair, etc. (the chair being in parallel perspective.) Then on the ground line, to the right of a, points l_1, q, l, m, n, o_1, o, and p are laid off from actual measurements from the plan. When these points are projected forwards to the vanishing line $a\,b_1$, the positions and widths of the bookcase, chair, large window, etc., are located. Vertical measurements are located in the usual way. The diagram is then converted into a picture by rendering it with pen and ink.

TYPICAL OBJECTS IN ANGULAR PERSPECTIVE

NOTE.—As he studies the descriptions of Figs. 13 to 19 the student is expected to make similar drawings. These drawings, however, are not to be sent to the Schools for examination; they are to be made simply for practice, and to make the descriptions given more easily understood.

32. Necessity for Accurate Drawing of Parts of a Picture.—It is not only important for the prospective illustrator to learn that entire scenes, exterior and interior views, must be laid out accurately according to the principles of perspective; he must also learn that every object or detail in such views or in his picture is subject to the same principles. For instance, in a street scene, not only the buildings, sidewalks, rails of the car tracks, and other stable objects, have definite vanishing points, but the vehicles, such as the cars, automobiles, wagons, carriages, etc., likewise have definite vanishing points. Similarly, the details of an interior scene, such as chairs, rugs, etc., have definite vanishing points, and must be drawn in accordance therewith.

33. Octagonal Prisms.—The octagonal prism may serve as a type of objects needed in nearly every picture. When placed below the horizon line, the top of the prism may serve as a table, a rug pattern, etc.; when placed above the horizon, it may typify a chandelier, a ceiling pattern, etc.

Two octagonal prisms, one above and the other below the horizon line, are shown in Fig. 13. The square containing the octagonal base is $2\frac{1}{2}$ inches on each side, and therefore on the measuring line $A\,B$, the distance $a\,b$ of $2\frac{1}{2}$ inches is laid off both to the left and to the right, of a. Distances $a\,d$ are laid off to the left and to the right from dimensions on

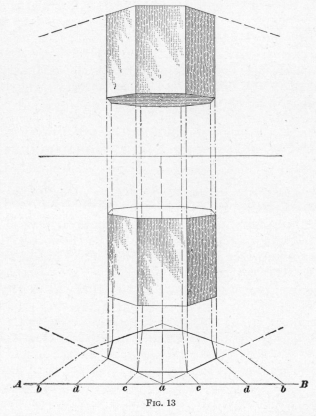

FIG. 13

the plan; that is, about $1\frac{3}{4}$ inches, as will be found by constructing a $2\frac{1}{2}$-inch square and an octagon within it, and then measuring the distance from one corner of the square, along one edge, to the farthest corner of the octagon on that edge; which distance is the same as one-half the diagonal of the enclosing square.

The vanishing points are 20 inches apart, but not shown in the figure. Lines are also drawn from *b*, *d*, and *c* toward the measuring points, which also are not shown in the figure; these lines intersect lines drawn from *a* toward the vanishing points, so as to lay out the octagon, as shown. This octagon serves as the base of the octagonal prism. The height of the prism may be determined as explained before, all vertical measurements being taken on a vertical measuring line erected at *a* and projected back properly to the other verticals.

34. Drawing a Perspective on a Narrow Sheet.—A drawing like that shown in Fig. 13 could be made upon a sheet of drawing paper as small as 6 inches wide by 9 inches high. In other words, there is no necessity for having the sheet 20 inches or more wide merely because the vanishing points are 20 inches apart. Fig. 14 illustrates how this may be done.

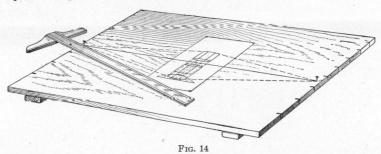

Fig. 14

A line may be drawn in ink on the drawing board to represent a horizon line, which can be used for any number of drawings. On this line may be located, at the proper places, the vanishing points, the measuring points, the center of vision, etc. Pins or headless tacks may be used as permanent vanishing points for simple drawings; in elaborate drawings, however, the positions of the vanishing points must be altered. The small drawing sheet could then be placed as shown in Fig. 14, and the perspective drawing made.

35. A Flight of Steps.—The necessity of a thorough training in perspective drawing is well shown when one attempts to draw a flight of steps, in perspective; especially a flight in which some of the steps are below and some are above the level of the eye. Without this training, such a flight cannot be drawn satisfactorily.

In the flight shown in Fig. 15, each step is 6 inches high, 10 inches wide, and 3 feet 6 inches long. To draw this flight, first the horizontal measuring line *A B* is drawn, then the perspective plan is laid off with the nearest corner *a* touching the measuring line. From *a*, to the right, the length *a b* of

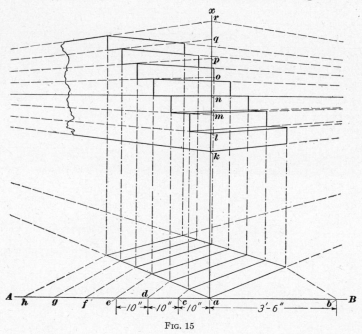

Fig. 15

each step, or 3 feet 6 inches, is laid off to scale, whatever scale is selected. To the left of *a*, on the ground line, *a c*, *c d*, *d e*, *e f*, *f g*, and *g h* are each laid off each 10 inches to scale, representing the depth of each tread of the steps. Lines drawn from these points to the measuring points will intersect with lines drawn from *a* to the vanishing points, and will give the points from which the perspective plan of the steps can be drawn, as shown. The vertical *a x* can then be erected at the point *a* where the perspective plan touches the measuring line, and thus becomes the measuring line for the heights of the steps. The distances $k\,l$, $l\,m$, $m\,n$, $n\,o$, $o\,p$, $p\,q$, and $q\,r$ are then laid off, each 6 inches, representing the heights of each of the risers of the steps. Lines drawn from these points to the left vanishing point will determine the perspective height, or the rise of each step and the perspective width, or tread of

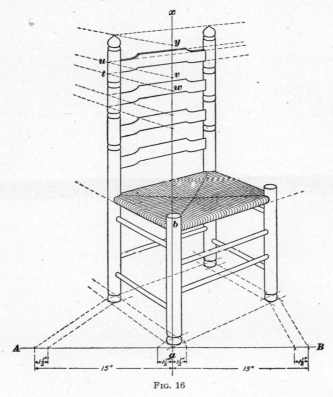

FIG. 16

each step can be projected up from the plan as shown. When this is done at the front side and the far side of the flight of steps, and then the proper edges of risers and treads are vanished toward the right vanishing point, the steps will be completed.

36. A Chair.—The necessity for the pictorial artist having a thorough training in perspective drawing is also shown in the case of a chair. As in the case of many other objects, though, it is only necessary to draw the skeleton in perspective; the covering and other details may then be drawn freehand. Fig. 16 shows the perspective drawing of a simple rush-seated chair with a slat back. In plan, the seat and legs may be enclosed within a square 15 inches on each side. As the diameter of the cylindrical legs of the chair is $1\frac{1}{2}$ inches, $1\frac{1}{2}$-inch squares can be laid off in each corner of the large 15-inch square. All this is accomplished by laying off the scaled dimensions on the measuring line $A\ B$ as shown, projecting back to the measuring points, thence to the vanishing points as previously explained.

37. The height $a\ b$ to the top of the front legs is 14 inches, and from the floor to the top of the seat 13 inches; the legs project 1 inch above the seat in front. The height of the rear legs, which are continued up to form the chair back, is 33 inches. This distance is laid off on the line $a\ x$, locating the height at y. Lines vanished from a and y to the left vanishing point will determine the height of the nearer rear leg (or back) of the chair, and a line vanished from the point thus obtained backwards toward the right vanishing point will locate the height of the farther rear leg (or back) upon a vertical erected at the far corner of the perspective plan. The positions of the slats of the back of the chair are also laid off on the line $a\ x$, as shown at v and w, and for those below. Their dimensions are projected to the chair back by lines to the left vanishing point, as shown at u and t. Lines from u and t vanished to the right show the position of the top slat across the back of the chair. The other slats are located in a similar manner, the irregular portions being put in freehand.

38. A Hall Clock.—In the case of the clock shown in Fig. 17, a simplified method of working is shown. The plans of the bottom, middle, and top sections are drawn just below each section, the rear lines of the plans coinciding, as shown in (b), and then the details of the clock are sketched in almost entirely freehand.

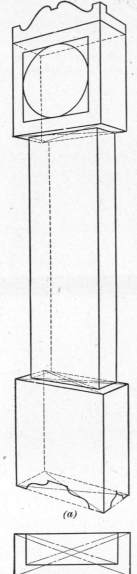

(a)

(b)

FIG. 17

I L T 22—6

By this method, pieces of furniture of this character can be rapidly introduced into a perspective drawing of an interior. In fact, for general work the whole perspective can be suggested freehand and the vanishing points assumed afterwards in such a position as to give the desired effect, and the whole drawing worked up accurately according to the preliminary freehand sketch.

39. Rendered Perspective of a House.—An illustrator is frequently required to draw a house, or other building, in perspective. No matter what the purpose of the drawing may be, whether for use in a catalog, a magazine, or a street-car advertisement, for an architect to show a client the appearance of a proposed building, etc., the drawing must be made in correct perspective.

As shown in Fig 18, a house may be constructed within an imaginary rectilinear solid, or solids, just as were the tents already drawn. If fully dimensioned floor and roof plans and elevations of the building are furnished, it is a simple matter to lay out the first-floor plan in perspective, as shown by the lower part of Fig. 18, and the second-floor plan in perspective, as shown by the second plan from the bottom. From these plans the horizontal measurements may be projected upwards to their proper positions in the perspective elevation above. The vertical measurements may be laid off above the ground line on the vertical $a\ x$ and projected backwards to the right and left vanishing points to locate their proper places. Lines yx, xu, uv, and vw indicate the top front edges of the various enclosing rectilinear solids in which the different wings of the house are considered as being constructed.

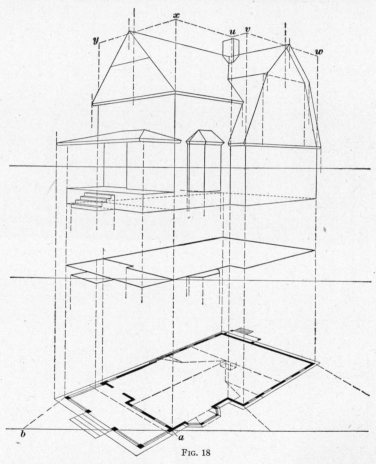

Fig. 18

40. When the skeleton of the perspective drawing has been completed, there is ample opportunity for the exercise of good draftsmanship, taste, and originality in clothing the perspective skeleton of the house with all the accessories it should possess, such as porch posts, doors, windows, trims,

lattice, etc., and to place about the house the proper landscape accessories of trees, bushes, grass, paths, distant hills,
sky, etc.

Fig. 19 shows a completed rendering, in pen and ink, of
the building drawn in perspective elevation in Fig. 18. To
relieve the harshness of the lines, and to make the rendering

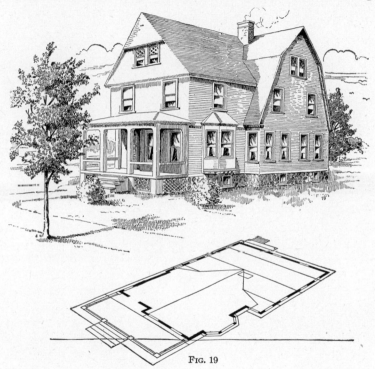

FIG. 19

as pictorial as possible, there are introduced landscape accessories, such as distant sky and clouds, trees, grass, bushes,
sidewalks, etc. A comparison of Figs. 18 and 19 will show
how far the skeleton outline needs to be carried, and how the
remainder of the work is purely freehand, giving opportunity
for the exercise of the highest artistic ability. It will thus be
seen that, in order to prepare a successful perspective rendering, the student need simply combine the training in rendering
he has already received with his present training in perspective.

OBLIQUE PERSPECTIVE

INTRODUCTION

41. So far, the perspective drawings have been confined to objects and scenes in which the lines are either vertical or horizontal to the ground plane. As a result, the vertical lines have remained vertical in the perspective view and the horizontal lines have been parallel to the picture planes or have vanished to some point on the horizon line. Most scenes and objects, however, contain some lines or planes that form an acute angle with the ground plane; these are in **oblique perspective.** Common examples of these are the roofs of houses, tents, etc. and partly opened lids of boxes, covers of books, etc.

LOCATING POINTS FOR OBLIQUE PARALLEL PERSPECTIVE

42. If the vanishing line or plane is horizontal, it vanishes somewhere on the horizon; therefore, if the line or plane is inclined it must vanish somewhere above or below the horizon. This is easily shown by placing a book upon a table with its bound edge toward the eye and parallel to the picture plane. The book will then be in parallel perspective and the two ends will vanish on the horizon line; the exact position of this vanishing point may be found by means of strings. If the top cover is opened, however, the strings will show that the ends will vanish in a point somewhere above the horizon line. It will also be found that the height of this point above the horizon line depends on the amount that the book is opened. As the cover vanishes at an angle, this consideration of oblique perspective may be understood as coming under the general head of angular perspective.

If the bound edge is placed away from the observer, when the top cover is opened, it will be found that the vanishing point of the ends is somewhere below the horizon line.

43. The times when the upper vanishing point or the lower vanishing point is to be used must be firmly fixed in mind.   The *upper* vanishing point must always be used when the edge is raised *away from* the observer; that is, when the bound edge of the book is toward the observer so that as the cover is raised it extends upwards and away from the observer.   The *lower* vanishing point must always be used when the edge is raised *toward* the observer; that is, when the bound edge of the book is away from the observer so that as the cover is raised it extends toward the observer, but when looked at vanishes downwards.

44. Locating Vanishing Points When Angle Opens Away From Observer.—Fig. 20 illustrates this experiment performed with the 2-foot box with hinged lid. If the box is placed squarely on the ground and the lid is raised about 1 foot or more, the top of the lid will take the position $a\,b$ shown in side view (a). When placed in parallel perspective, as in perspective view (b), it will be noticed that the edges of the lid will vanish somewhere above the point $V\,P$; namely, in an upper vanishing point $U\,V\,P$, and on the vertical center line. Just how far above the horizon this point must be placed depends on the angle at which the lid is raised.

If the lid is raised at an angle of 45°, as shown in side view (a), a line must be drawn, in view (b), from $M\,P$ (*Right*) upwards and inwards toward the vertical center line, and at an angle of 45° with the horizon line, until it intersects the vertical center line at $U\,V\,P$. This point will be the vanishing point for the inclined long edges of the box lid. The short (side) edges of the thickness of the lid will vanish at a corresponding point $L\,V\,P$ below the horizon, because these edges are at right angles with the long top edges. In this way oblique parallel perspective is shown.

45. It is not enough merely to learn the direction of the vanishing lines; their extent must also be determined. To do this, the indefinite vertical line $k\,e$, Fig. 20 (b), is used as the vertical measuring line. Points a and c of view (a) are projected over to it, locating a_1 and c_1, then upwards and backwards toward $V\,P$ until the line from c_1 cuts the vanishing line $g\,U\,V\,P$, the under side of the raised lid, thus locating

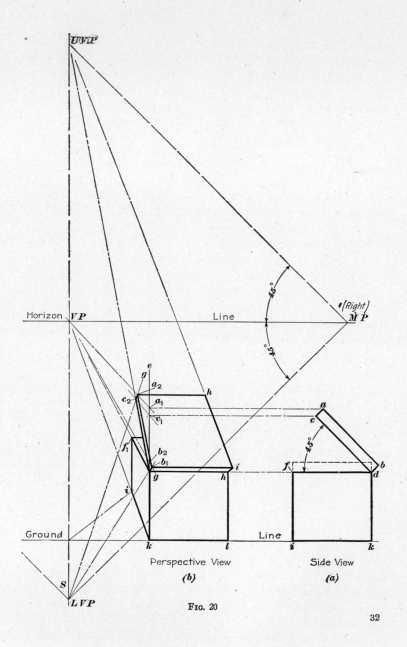

Fig. 20

Perspective View
(b)

Side View
(a)

point c_2. A line from $L\ V\ P$ is projected up through c_2 indefinitely. The upper right corner a_2 of the raised lid is found by projecting a_1 back toward $V\ P$ until its line cuts the vanishing line $LVP\ g$ at a_2. Other corners h, i, and b_1 of the raised lid in oblique perspective are found in the same manner.

46. If the box were to remain in parallel perspective, and the lid were to open toward the side, there would be no need of locating the upper and lower vanishing points, because the long edges of the inclined lid of the box would be parallel to the picture plane, and would therefore be laid off directly at the specified angle (say 45°) and then drawn parallel, the upper edge vanishing at $V\ P$.

47. Locating Vanishing Points When Angle Opens Toward Observer.—If the hinges are at the back of the box and the opening edge at the front, when the lid is raised its long edges will vanish below the horizon, at the point $L\ V\ P$, because when the lid is so raised the front edge is nearer to the observer, therefore apparently longer, than the rear hinged edge.

LOCATING POINTS FOR OBLIQUE ANGULAR PERSPECTIVE

48. Locating Vanishing Points When Angle Opens Away From Observer.—As an example of oblique angular perspective, suppose that three boxes are arranged in angular perspective but that the lids are inclined upwards and away from the observer, as shown in Fig. 21 (b). The upper and lower vanishing points will not then be on the center line but on a vertical line passing through the right or left vanishing point, as the case may be; that is, through $V\ P$ (*Right*) or $V\ P$ (*Left*). The position of this line depends on whether the lids open toward the right or toward the left. The upper and lower vanishing points are found, as in oblique parallel perspective, by running 45° lines up from the right or the left measuring points. In oblique angular perspective, however, these lines will not cut the center line $S\ c$ extended, because in angular perspective there is no vanishing point on that line. But, as

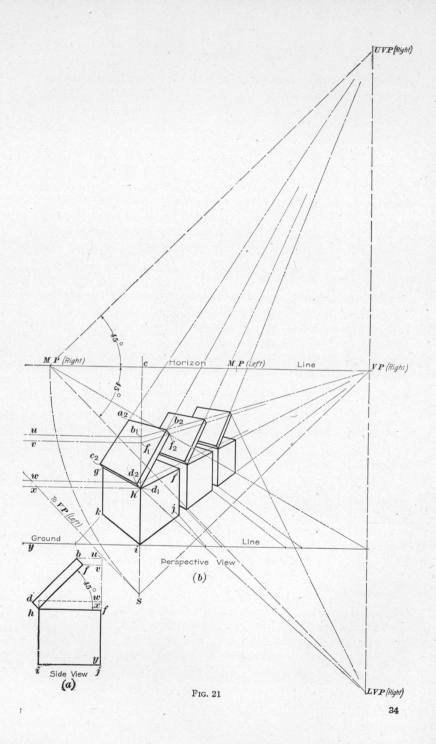

UVP (Right)

M P (Right)   c   Horizon   *M P (Left)*   Line   *VP (Right)*

45°

45°

a_2

b_2

b_1

u

v

f_1 f_2

c_2

w

g

x

d_2

To **VP** (Left)

h d_1

f

k

j

Ground   Line

y

i

Perspective View

b   u

(b)

f   v

45°

d

w

x   f

h

y

i   Side View   j

s

(a)

FIG. 21

34

shown in Fig. 21, these 45° lines will cut a vertical line drawn through $V P$ (*Right*).

49. In Fig. 21 (*b*), the long edges $c_2 a_2$ and $d_2 b_2$ of the inclined lid of the nearest box will vanish at $U V P$ (*Right*), because they extend upwards, away from the observer, and toward the right. The short edges $c_2 g$ and $d_2 h$ which show the thickness of the lid, extend downwards, away from the observer, and toward the right, and therefore vanish at $L V P$ (*Right*). Edges $a_2 b_2$ and $c_2 d_2$ vanish on the horizon at $V P$ (*Left*) because they remain parallel with the ground; that is, they remain horizontal. If the open lids of the boxes extended upwards and toward the left their long edges would vanish at $U V P$ (*Left*) and the short edges that show the thickness of lid would vanish at $L V P$ (*Left*). The horizontal edges of the raised lid would then vanish on the horizon at $V P$ (*Right*). The method of obtaining the vertical measurements in such an angular perspective view is to draw a side view as in (*a*), place its base line $i j$ on a level with the ground line y, lay off vertical dimensions on $j u$, and project them over to the right, on to vertical measuring line $i c$, in perspective view (*b*), thence back to the proper vanishing points.

50. Locating Vanishing Points When Angle Opens Toward Observer.—Assuming that the bodies of the boxes remain as shown in Fig. 21, but that the hinges are at the rear and the open parts are at the fronts of the boxes, then the long edges of the raised lids will vanish at $L V P$ (*Right*) because they extend downwards, away from, and toward the right. The short edges, which show the thickness of the lid, will vanish at $U V P$ (*Right*), because they extend upwards, away from, and toward the right.

If the boxes are turned so that the lids open toward the left, but with the hinges at the rear and the open part at the front of the box, the long edges will vanish at $L V P$ (*Left*), because they extend downwards, away from, and toward the left. The short edges, which show the thickness of the lid, will vanish at $U V P$ (*Left*), because they extend upwards, away from, and toward the left. The student should supplement these explanations by making experiments with a book and its open cover, or a cigar box and its open lid, the object being placed as directed in the foregoing explanations.

MAKING AN OBLIQUE PERSPECTIVE DRAWING

NOTE.—As he studies the descriptions of Figs. 22 and 23 the student is expected to make a similar drawing. The drawing, however, is not to be sent to the Schools for examination; it is to be made simply for practice and to make the descriptions given more easily understood.

51. **Typical Application of Oblique Perspective.** Except for finding the upper and lower vanishing points, no new element enters into the making of oblique perspective drawings. This is shown in the group of houses in Figs. 22 and 23. These houses are at a street corner and most of their roofs slope at an angle of 45°; a few of the roof sections slope at lesser angles.

Fig. 22 shows a group of houses viewed in 45° perspective by a person standing on the opposite corner of the street intersection. Of course, the roofs could have been constructed within imaginary solids, as were the roofs of the tents, and the roof of the house in Fig. 18, but, many times, roofs and other inclined planes must be accurately drawn. This can only be done by vanishing these planes to their proper vanishing points.

52. As the methods of drawing the plans and the rectilinear portions of the houses have been fully explained, the chief problem here is drawing the roofs. The first step is to determine which are the front and which are the rear parts of the roofs. The front, or nearer parts, always vanish at an upper vanishing point, because they extend upwards and away from the observer. If they extend toward the left, as in the case of houses A and B, they vanish at $U\,V\,P$ (*Left*), if they extend toward the right, as in the cases of house C, they vanish at $U\,V\,P$ (*Right*). The other, or rear, parts of the roofs, because they extend downwards and away from the observer, vanish at lower vanishing points. If these **rear** parts extend toward the left, as in the case of houses A

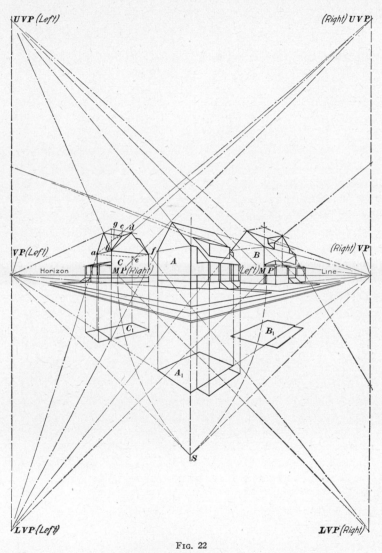

FIG. 22

37

and B, they vanish at $L V P$ (*Left*); if they extend toward
the right, as in the case of house C, they vanish at $L V P$ (*Right*).

**53. Drawing Roof Slopes Toward Proper Vanishing
Points.**—It is assumed that all parts of house C, for instance,
are drawn up to the line $a b f$ of the eaves. To draw the front
roof slope, part of which, $c d b$, is visible, the same procedure is
followed as in drawing the lid of the first box in Fig. 21. Point
$U V P$ (*Right*) is located on the vertical line through $V P$ (*Right*)
by running a 45° line upwards from $M P$ (*Right*) to meet
the right-hand vertical. Point $U V P$ (*Left*) is located similarly
by running a 45° line upwards from $M P$ (*Left*) to cut vertical
erected through $V P$ (*Left*). Points $L V P$ (*Right*) and
$L V P$ (*Left*) are found by running the 45° lines downwards
instead of upwards.

To draw the front roof slope of house C, of which the portion
$b c d$, is visible, lines are drawn from a and b to $U V P$ (*Right*).
To locate the slope of the rear part of the roof of house C,
lines are drawn up from $L V P$ (*Right*) through e and f to
cut lines $a U V P$ (*Right*) and $b U V P$ (*Right*), at g and d;
$g d$ thus becomes the ridge line of that section of the roof.
The other parts of the roof, namely the front and rear gables,
are drawn in a similar manner, except that the slopes vanish
at $U V P$ (*Left*) and $L V P$ (*Left*).

54. The front part of the roofs of the houses A and B,
vanish upwards and to the left, therefore at $U V P$ (*Left*),
and the rear roof slopes vanish downwards and to the left,
therefore at $L V P$ (*Left*). It will be observed that the
angles of the slopes of the projecting gambrel roof on house A
and the dormer on house B are at still different angles; the
points, however, are obtained, as before, on vertical lines
through $V P$ (*Left*) and $V P$ (*Right*). The methods described
for drawing these roof slopes will cover any class of roof slopes
with which the illustrator may meet.

55. Pictorial Rendering of Group of Houses.—In
Fig. 23 is shown a pictorial rendering of Fig. 22. This is
introduced to show how the skeleton lines of Fig. 22 are all
that need be drawn accurately in perspective and that the

Fig. 23

rest of the work on the finished picture can be done entirely freehand and with as much artistic finish as may be desired.

This pictorial rendering, as well as the others shown, emphasizes the fact that the pictorial artist must know just where every line and plane in his picture vanishes, otherwise he cannot properly lay out the directions and locations of these lines and planes, and thus the drawing of his picture will not be correct. If the proportioning and drawing of the objects and details in his picture are not correct, no amount of skilful rendering, or of so-called artistic touches, can make it successful.

PERSPECTIVE OF CIRCLES AND CURVES

56. Projecting Curves on to the Picture Plane. There has been considered so far only the perspective drawing of straight lines; and their vanishing points can always be located by looking in the direction of the lines and observing where they pierce the picture plane. With curved lines, however, an entirely different condition of affairs is met. Because

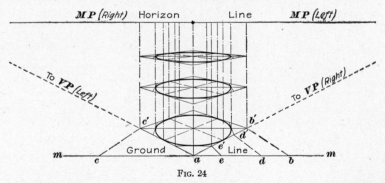

Fig. 24

of their changing direction, they may not come in contact with the picture plane at all, but may remain entirely beyond it. Lines of sight from the eye of the spectator to the contour of the curves, however, will pierce the picture plane in such a manner as to locate a number of points that can be connected and represent the perspective of the arc or the circle, as the case may be.

57. In drawing circles in perspective, no serious difficulty will be met if they are always considered as polygons having an infinite number of sides drawn within a rectangle. For example, a square can be drawn in a position similar to that of the circle and then projected in perspective. If desired, this square may afterwards be converted into an octagon and then into a sixteen-sided figure, by locating on the sides of the square (and octagon) the points in perspective where the extra sides will intersect. In the majority of cases, the sixteen-sided figure will be so near a circle that it will require

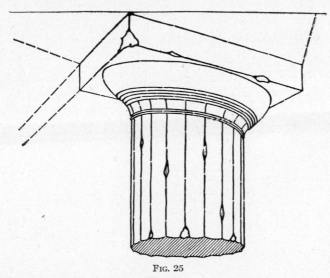

Fig. 25

simply a gentle curving of the lines in order to produce the ellipse that represents the circle in perspective.

58. Horizontal Circles in Perspective.—When studying the foreshortening of the cylinder, cone, etc., it was found that, when seen in perspective, a circular shape appears elliptic. It was also found that, if the circle is horizontal, more of the surface will be seen the farther it is placed below the level of the eye.

Fig. 24 illustrates graphically the relative amounts of surface of a horizontal disk or circular shape that can be seen as the

circle is lowered below or raised to the eye level The first
step in laying out a circle in perspective (after the station
point, vanishing points, measuring points, horizon line, measuring line, etc., have been located), is to place the circle within
a square.   Distances *a b* and *a c* equal to the side of the
square are then laid off on the ground line *m m*.   By projecting
the distance *a b* back to *M P* (*Right*), *b′* is located on the right-
hand vanishing line *a V P* (*Right*).   By projecting the distance *a c* back to *M P* (*Left*), *c′* is located on the left-hand

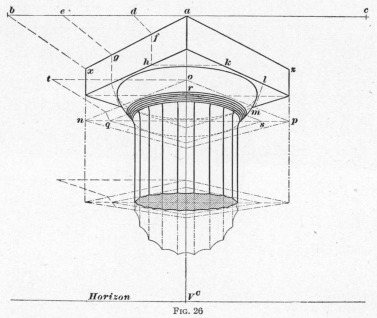

FIG. 26

vanishing line *a V P* (*Left*).   It simply remains then to vanish
lines back from *b′* and *c′* to *V P* (*Left*) and *V P* (*Right*),
respectively; their point of intersection will form the rear
corner of the square in perspective.   The ellipse may now
be sketched in freehand as shown.

It is sometimes helpful to construct an octagon within the
square, as shown in the illustration, and then round off
the corners of the octagon to secure the ellipse representing the circle in perspective.

59. As this circle is raised toward the horizon line (the eye level) less and less of its surface is shown and the ellipse becomes flatter and flatter. When it reaches the eye level, instead of appearing as an ellipse, the circle appears as a straight line.

60.   Avoiding Distorted Views.—In making perspective drawings of horizontal circles it is always best to consider them as exactly in the center of vision. When they are moved far to the right or left the ellipses (showing circles in perspective) are likely to become greatly distorted unless the drawing is so held that the object shown appears at its proper distance to the right or left of the eye. As an example, the angular

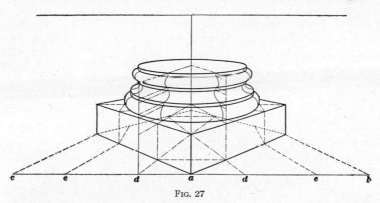

FIG. 27

perspective drawing of the upper part of the column, its capital, and the slab it supports, in Fig. 25, appears very greatly distorted, because it is very much to the left and above the center of vision. No matter how the column and capital may be placed in the scene being drawn, the correct method of drawing them is that shown in Fig. 26; that is, as if they were in 45° perspective exactly opposite the eye; then no distortion would occur.

61. In Figs. 27 and 28 are shown two methods of drawing the base of a column and the slab upon which it rests so that the ellipses are not distorted. In Fig. 27, the entire drawing is in 45° perspective, but in Fig. 28, the supporting slab is

I L T 22—7

drawn as it might appear, say, quite far to the left of the center of vision. The moldings of the circular base, however, are drawn as if the base were directly in front of the eye; that is, in 45° perspective, thus preventing all appearances of distortion.

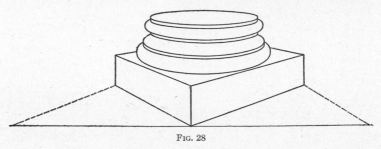

FIG. 28

62. Vertical Circles in Perspective.—When the circle is in a vertical position, the ellipse is drawn, the same as the horizontal ellipse, by placing it in a foreshortened vertical square, as shown in Fig. 29. In this case, an outline drawing

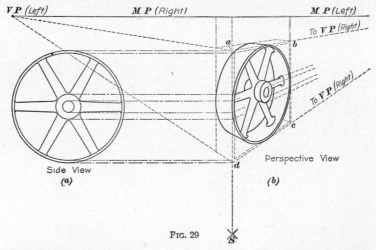

FIG. 29

of an iron pulley wheel is made. As shown, the circle representing the rim of the wheel is considered as being enclosed in a square box, *a b c d.* The perspective of this square box appears as a rectangular box, inasmuch as the wheel has considerable thickness, and two ellipses are drawn for the rim—one

in front of the box and the other at the rear. The hub of the
wheel is constructed in a smaller rectangular box. The lines
that connect the ellipses at the top and bottom of the wheel,
and represent the thickness or breadth of the rim, are drawn
toward $V P$ (*Left*) as shown.

The method of securing the perspective measurements of
the wheel follows the same principle as that used for the
horizontal circle. The height $a d$, Fig. 29, may be laid off
direct, or projected from the side view (a), and then carried
back toward $V P$ (*Right*) becoming $b c$ at the right-hand side
of wheel. The width $d c$ is first laid off on the measuring
line and then projected back to $M P$ (*Right*) to cut the vanishing line $d V P$ (*Right*). The depth of the enclosing box, and
therefore of the wheel, is secured on the same principle.

63. It is important that the principles of placing a wheel
in perspective should be thoroughly understood. In pictorial
work, though, the actual measurements are not so important
as the correct application of the principles. In all cases,
the wheel should first of all be placed in an imaginary box
and this box should be drawn in perspective.

64. Other applications of the principles governing the
drawing of vertical circles in perspective are shown in the
drawing of a round-top window, an arch, a series of arches,
etc. The method of drawing these is shown in Fig. 30. In
the example shown, the plan gives no data for the proportioning of the curve except its perspective diameter. However,
in constructing the perspective view (a), there is given, in
perspective, a parallelogram $a b c d$ that is the perspective
representation of the parallelogram $a' b' c' d'$, view (b), that
contains the semicircular arch of the opening.

The lines through the corners of this parallelogram that
give the octagon shape are located from the plan by laying
off the points on the measuring line $m m$, view (a), and projecting upwards to the top line $b c$ of the rectangle in which
the semiellipse is to be drawn. The point e, on the left side $a b$
of the rectangle in the perspective view, may be located by
marking off its true height $a_1 e_1$ on the nearest corner $x y$ of

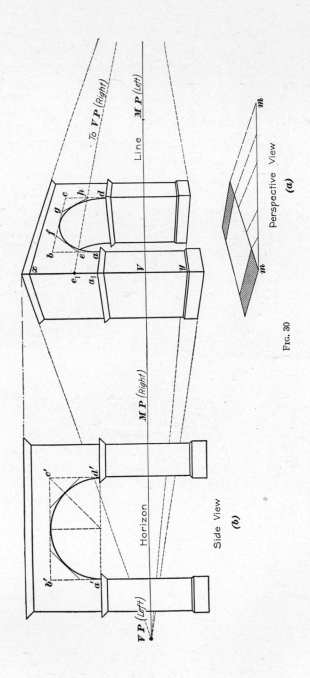

To V P (Right)

Line M P (Left)

x
g c
f b
e d
b
e₁
a₁
V
y

M P (Right)

Horizon

V P (Left)

Side View

(b)

c'
a'
b'
a'

Perspective View

(a)

m
m

Fig. 30

the archway, which is the vertical measuring line and is in contact with the picture plane. This height $a_1 e_1$ should then be projected to its true place on line $a\, b$ by vanishing it back toward $V\, P$ (*Right*), as shown. Point h, at the right-hand side $c\, d$ of the perspective rectangle is located by vanishing a line from e back to $V\, P$ (*Right*) and noting where it cuts $c\, d$. Thus, short lines $a\, e$, $e\, f$, $f\, g$, $g\, h$, and $h\, d$ can be drawn, which will complete the semioctagon. The semiellipse from a to d can then be sketched in freehand without any trouble. All the straight vertical and horizontal lines of the arch structure are drawn in according to the principles of angular perspective.

65. Curved Forms Other Than Circles in Perspective.—In practical work the illustrator will occasionally be required to place arbitrary curves in perspective; as, for instance, a roadway, a railroad, or a stream, starting somewhere in the foreground and winding off into the distance, getting narrower as it gets farther into the background. Other irregular curves or curved surfaces will have to be drawn from time to time by the illustrator. All such curved forms, however, are drawn by giving them a general rectangular form such as a square, rectangle, or other straight-line form, or a meshwork of squares and rectangles, and then placing these enclosing forms in perspective and sketching in the curved forms freehand upon the rectangular network as a basis. Methods of doing such work, particularly as to bird's-eye views, will be explained more in detail in *Pictorial Perspective*.

As a matter of fact, the principle of first basing all curved lines on straight lines, curved surfaces on straight surfaces, and curved solids on rectilinear solids, before placing them in perspective, will enable one to block in, freehand, the most difficult combinations of shapes and forms in perspective. Cones, cylinders, spheres, as well as irregularly shaped lines, planes and solids, can thus be blocked in with the greatest accuracy. Even the human figure itself is first so blocked in when foreshortening it. If freehand perspective for pictorial purposes is handled on these principles, there need never be any difficulty experienced by the illustrator.

PERSPECTIVE DRAWING EXERCISES

GENERAL INFORMATION

66. Required Work in Angular Perspective.—The only satisfactory test to determine whether one understands how to lay out a drawing in angular perspective is to make such a drawing. While it is assumed that the diagrams illustrating the various classes of angular perspective have been drawn, no original perspective drawings have yet been prepared. Therefore, the work in this subject will consist of exercises arranged as four drawing plates, each one 20 inches wide by 15 inches high, which is the full size of the regular 15″×20″ sheet of cold-pressed white drawing paper. These plates are to be sent to the Schools for inspection in the manner directed, and while each plate is being examined and returned, the student will be working on the following plate.

67. Preliminary Practice Work (Not To Be Sent In).—On a sheet of white paper of the usual size arranged horizontally, make an outline pencil drawing in 45° angular perspective of the three boxes shown in Fig. 2, each box standing on the ground and being 2 feet by 2 feet by 2 feet, and 6 inches from its neighbor. The observer is to be 20 feet away from the right-hand corner of the nearest box. The scale of the objects is to be $\frac{1}{2}$ in. = 1 ft.; as to points, S in the drawing may be 10 inches below the horizon line, which line will be 20 inches long and placed about $2\frac{1}{2}$ inches below the top edge of the sheet of drawing paper. The vanishing points will then be 20 inches apart and the measuring points will be located as already described.

This preliminary work, which is done to become familiar with the principles of angular perspective, is NOT to be sent in to the Schools. The only work to be submitted is that of the Plates bearing numbers and described later.

68. Character of the Drawing Plates.—It is understood, of course, that none of the drawings made by the student are to be, in any respect, copies of any illustration, in this subject; they must be original. While they are along the same lines as those in the text, the specified distances of points, etc., must be purposely altered, as will be seen. All measurements of objects are to be taken direct (to scale) from those given in the text illustrations referred to, and may therefore be laid off on the proper measuring line. Therefore, no top or plan views and side views need be laid out. In making any angular perspective drawing it is well to keep the vanishing points (for these plates) at least 20 inches apart, thus avoiding distortion of nearest parts. For example, in doing Plate 4, the points *MP, VP* (*right*), *UVP* (*right*), *LVP* (*right*), of Fig. 21, should all be laid out quite far apart—even if on the drawing board, see Fig. 14: the *scale* of the boxes remaining as directed.

PLATE 1

69. Exercise for Plate 1.—On the sheet arranged horizontally, make an outline pencil drawing in 60° and 30° angular perspective of the three boxes shown in Fig. 3. The same conditions as to size of boxes, distance away of the observer, scale of making drawing, etc., are to apply as applied in the practice work described in Art. **67,** but the drawing will resemble that in Fig. 3, and the horizon line will be longer than the horizon line in Art. **67.** (It would be well first to sketch in freehand the plan of the three boxes so that the vanishing points can be properly located.)

All vanishing points, vanishing lines, and construction lines, should be drawn clearly and distinctly and should be allowed to remain; nothing should be erased. The outlines of the objects themselves should be drawn somewhat heavier, with a sharp-pointed soft pencil.

70. Final Work on Plate 1.—Letter or write the title, Plate 1: Angular Perspective, at the top of the sheet, and on the back, at the lower left-hand corner, place class letters and number, name, address, and date of completing the plate. Roll the plate, place in the mailing tube, and send to the Schools for inspection. Then proceed with Plate 2.

PLATE 2

71. Exercise for Plate 2.—On the sheet arranged horizontally, make an outline drawing in angular perspective of the two rows of tents shown in Fig. 6. The vertical and horizontal measurements of tents, street, etc., should be the same as are shown in top view (a), side view (b), and front view (c). The observer S is to be 30 feet away from d_2, of top view (a), the nearest corner of the first tent in the right-hand row. Make scale of the objects $\frac{1}{4}$ in. $=1$ ft.; and make the horizon line 15 or more actual inches long on the drawing and S will be placed $7\frac{1}{2}$ or more actual inches below it. No top view of the tents will be needed, as in (a), because these tents are to be laid out from actual scaled measurements. Do not erase any lines after drawing is made.

72. Final Work on Plate 2.—Letter or write the title, Plate 2: Angular Perspective, at the top of the sheet, and on the back, at the lower left-hand corner, place class letters and number, name and address, and the date of completing the plate. Roll the plate, place in the mailing tube, and send to the Schools for inspection. If all required redrawn work on previous plates has been completed, proceed with Plate 3.

Attention is again called to the fact that the dimensions for this problem have been purposely changed from those of Fig. 6, and the drawing will therefore differ from Fig. 6 in some respects.

PLATE 3

73. Exercise for Plate 3.—On the sheet arranged horizontally, make an outline pencil drawing in angular perspective of the room interior, after the method shown in Fig. 8, where the picture plane is arbitrarily placed at the rear corner of the room. Select a suitable scale for the drawing, which may be $\frac{1}{4}$ in. $=1$ ft., $\frac{1}{2}$ in. $=1$ ft., or even 1 in. $=1$ ft., depending on the size of the sheet used. It may be necessary to use a 15″×20″ sheet, or even two 15″×20″ sheets pasted together on the two long edges, but the drawing of the room interior should be at least 4 inches square or thereabouts.

The completed drawing will resemble Fig. 8 in its method of construction with the following change: The two windows and desk (appearing in Fig. 8 on the right-hand side) must be placed at rear (left) wall; and the door (appearing in Fig. 8 in rear wall) must be placed in right-hand side wall. All vanishing lines, points, etc., must be allowed to remain. Nothing is to be erased. No dimensions need be placed on the drawing.

74. Final Work on Plate 3.—Letter or write the title, Plate 3: Angular Perspective, at the top of the sheet, and on the back, at the lower left-hand corner, place class letters and number, name and address, and the date of completing the plate. Roll the plate, place in the mailing tube, and send to the Schools for inspection. If all required redrawn work on previous plates has been completed, proceed with Plate 4.

PLATE 4

75. Exercise for Plate 4.—On the sheet arranged horizontally, make an outline pencil drawing in oblique angular perspective of the three boxes with lids upraised at an angle of 45°, shown in Fig. 21. The same conditions as to size of boxes, distance away of the observer, scale of making the drawing, etc., are to apply as applied in Art. **67.** In order to get upper and lower vanishing points within the vertical limits of the sheet, the 15″×20″ sheet may be pinned horizontally on the drawing board held vertically, so that some of the wood of the board shows above and below the sheet. The upper and lower right vanishing points may then be located on the wood of the board on a long vertical line through the right vanishing point, extended upwards and downwards beyond the top and bottom edges of the sheet. This 15″×20″ sheet may be used, even though not accommodating all the points and lines. All vanishing points, lines, etc., must be allowed to remain. Nothing is to be erased.

Reference must again be made to the advisability of keeping the vanishing points at least 20 actual inches apart, and the objects near (or on) the horizon, to avoid distortion in the nearest objects.

76. Final Work on Plate 4.—Letter or write the title, Plate 4: Angular Perspective, at the top of the sheet, and on the back, at the lower left-hand corner, place class letters and number, name and address, and the date of completing the plate. Roll the plate, place in the mailing tube, and send to the Schools for inspection.

If any redrawn work on any of the plates of this subject has been called for, and has not yet been completed, it should be satisfactorily finished at this time. After all required work on the plates of this subject has been completed, the work of the next subject, in which both parallel and angular perspective are applied pictorially, should be taken up at once.

PICTORIAL PERSPECTIVE

Perspective Used to Show Realism in a Pictorial View

PICTORIAL PERSPECTIVE

Serial 1729-3

————

Edition 1

PERSPECTIVE IN PICTORIAL WORK

————

PERSPECTIVE IN NATURE SKETCHING

1. Application of Perspective to Freehand Sketching.—As already shown, a clear working knowledge of perspective principles is necessary before any one can sketch from nature or prepare commercial illustrations, newspaper illustrations and cartoons, or magazine and book illustrations. Without this knowledge, he cannot draw exactly the various parts of the sketch, diagram, illustration, or picture in their proper relation of size and position.

2. It is neither necessary nor desirable to draw a sketch or a composition picture, line for line, diagrammatically, like the examples that have so far been drawn in parallel and in angular perspective. Rather, such sketches and composition pictures should be drawn and rendered freehand, but care must be taken that no part of the drawing violates the rules of perspective. Suppose, for instance, that a street scene is to be sketched or put in a picture. It would not be practical for the artist to walk the full length of the street in order to measure the length and width of the street and to determine the position, width, depth, and height of each building, street car, tree, or other object on the street. Neither is this necessary. When the vanishing and measuring points and the horizon, ground, and vanishing lines are known, the street, buildings, trees, etc. can be blocked in freehand. All vertical and horizontal measurements may be estimated by eye measurement, and projected toward their proper measuring and vanishing points. In this way, with very few lines and in quite a short time, an accurate freehand perspective outline will have been constructed, which will serve as a skeleton or framework upon which the detailed rendering of the picture can be based.

Without this framework, it will be impossible to make a realistic drawing. A careful study of published illustrations of all kinds will show that the artists whose work is considered the best are those who have mastered the principles of perspective and apply them to their work.

3. Proper Selection and Arrangement of View. The term *nature sketching*, as used here, means any drawing or sketch made direct from the scene, whether that scene is in the streets of a city or town or in the fields and woods.

In all cases, the first consideration is to determine how much of the scene is to be included in the picture. For this purpose a *finder* should be used. This is simply a sheet of cardboard, say 10 in. × 12 in., in which a 6″×8″ hole has been cut. Through this finder, or frame, any part of the scene can be viewed, as through a picture frame, and thus selected for the picture.

4. When selecting the scene to be drawn, care must be taken to select such portions of the landscape or view as are well proportioned to the opening of the finder. A tall house, tower, or tree, for instance, should be viewed with the long side of the finder vertical and the object should be at one side of the picture. A landscape, showing many details spread out horizontally should be viewed with the long side of the finder horizontal. Stiff symmetrical positions of vertical lines in the picture should be avoided, as well as vanishing lines that make equal angles with the sides or bottom and top of the picture. If this position of the vanishing lines cannot be avoided, the straight lines and angles should be clothed, or partly covered, by trees, etc., if an exterior view, or by some article of furniture in an interior view. The finder thus serves to determine the limits of the picture, and the relations of the horizon and principal vanishing lines to these outlines or limits.

The proportionate shape of this finder or frame should be drawn on the paper on which the sketch is to be made as a basis upon which to lay out the sketch.

5. Locating Horizon and Vanishing Lines, Vanishing Points, Etc.—Let it be supposed that what is seen through the finder is the street scene shown in Fig. 1. The first procedure in making the drawing is to locate the horizon line. This may be done by means of the measuring string, as previously described, or by holding one edge of the sketching paper, or sketch block, horizontally. In the latter case, the paper should be raised until it encounters in the scene details that make a straight horizontal line, which will be somewhere along the masonry lines of the first story of the buildings. This horizon line should then be drawn as $E\,F$ in the rectangle $A\,B\,C\,D$, Fig. 2.

This horizon line may be placed at any desired position horizontally in the rectangle. Ordinarily, it is about one-third the distance above the bottom line. However, in a scene like this, where there are high buildings, it should be only about one-fourth the distance, as shown. The scene shown in Fig. 1 is manifestly in parallel perspective, but to avoid the vanishing lines making equal angles with the edges of the picture, the observer has moved to the left of the center of the picture; so that he sees more of the buildings on the right than of those on the left. As a result, there is only one vanishing point, which is found by testing with the pencil or a string, extending the vanishing lines of the sidewalk, ground line, window lines of all the buildings, cornices, etc., backwards until they cut the horizon at the same point. These lines should then be lightly sketched on the paper, as shown by the lines from the points a, b, c, d, e, f, g, h, i, j, k, l. m, etc., toward the point $V\,P$, on the horizon, in Fig. 2.

6. Plotting Positions and Sizes of Main Features. Next, the position of the main building on the right and the

FIG. 1

4

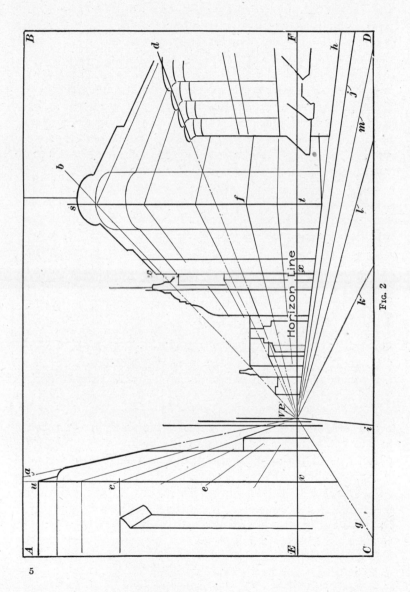

Fig. 2

Horizon Line

one in the left foreground should be located with relation to the vanishing lines and to the border lines $A\,C$ and $B\,D$. By imagining vertical lines to be drawn at the near corner lines of these two buildings and by using proportionate measurements with pencil and thumb nail held at arm's length, it will be found that the corner of the right-hand building is about one-third of the width of the finder from the right-hand edge $B\,D$, and the corner of the left-hand building about midway between the vanishing point and the left-hand edge $A\,C$. These two lines can then be plotted in as verticals $s\,t$ and $u\,v$, respectively.

The height above the horizon of the nearest vertical corner edges, $s\,t$ and $u\,v$ of the right-hand and the left-hand buildings can readily be determined by pencil and thumb-nail measurement and by comparison with verticals $B\,F$ and $A\,E$ respectively. Thus $s\,t$ is about two-thirds as long as BF; and $u\,v$ about seven-eighths as long as AE. In the same way, the perspective width of the main building on the right may be measured as being about one-third the distance from t to $V\,P$, and thus vertical $w\,x$ may be located.

The vanishing lines, positions and horizontal and vertical dimensions of all buildings and objects in the picture, may be plotted in the same way, thus forming the framework, or perspective skeleton, upon which the completed rendering of the picture may be built up.

In doing the freehand proportioning of lines, by means of pencil and thumb-nail measurements, the finder may be held in the left hand at the proper position, and the measuring pencil held in the right hand and at arm's length.

7. Aerial Perspective.—The ability of the artist to measure the sizes and distances apart of objects in a picture by means of eye measurements and relative proportions, and then to draw them in linear perspective, can apply only to objects reasonably near. Objects or details in the far distance cannot be so estimated, because their actual and relative sizes are not known. To correctly portray them, the illustrator depends on **aerial perspective,** which is the proper diminution of the strength of light, shade, and colors of objects according to their distances, the light falling on them, and the medium through which they are seen.

Suppose that a landscape, about to be sketched, includes some buildings surrounded by trees in the foreground, a clump of trees about ½ mile away, and another clump about 1 mile away. While the individual trees in each clump will appear much the same, there will be a marked difference in the appearance of each group. The nearest trees will be quite distinct; those ½ mile away will have a middle tone value, those 1 mile away will be faint in tone values. If there should be a range of hills in the extreme distance, say 4 or 5 miles away, these would appear as a faint outline on the horizon.

8. The relative dimness, or lack of sharpness of outline, and the relative lightening of tone value, are exactly proportionate in intensity to the distance away of the objects. If the near trees are rendered with a depth of green (or other value) that might be called 3, the ½-mile trees will require a tone value of but 2, and the 1-mile trees a value of only 1. In this way aerial perspective helps out linear perspective.

This is clearly shown in Fig. 10. The clothing of the soldier in the foreground is rendered quite dark, which might be called tone 3; that of the marching soldiers does not seem quite as dark and so may be called tone 2; while that of the soldier in front of the nearest tent appears again as light and may be called tone 1. The tents and other details in the landscape lose their sharpness of definition and lighten in tone value, the farther they recede from the eye.

9. A strange effect of aerial perspective is the change it produces in the apparent hues of the colors of objects. All dark objects appear much lighter and bluer in color while all light objects appear warmer in color. Perfectly white objects, however, are little affected by distance. When the sun is near the horizon, directly overhead the sky appears blue because the blue and violet rays of the sun's spectrum are reflected directly to the eye from the apparently pure air above. Toward the horizon, though, the color of the sky seems to get warmer because the atmosphere is more dense (that is, filled with dust, moisture, etc.) and the longer or heat waves of the solar light penetrate to the observer. In the morning or evening, a person looking directly toward the horizon will see only the red waves. For the same reason, distant mountains in shadow and the shaded side of distant trees that are known to be green, appear bluish-violet in color. The artist should therefore always paint distant objects or details in exactly the color he sees them and not in what he knows to be their local colors.

PERSPECTIVE IN COMMERCIAL ILLUSTRATING

MAKING A BIRD'S-EYE VIEW

10. Application of Perspective to Commercial Illustrating.—The classification *commercial illustrating* covers a wide range of work, but it is applied usually to lines of art work that assist in advertising and selling commodities, street-car cards, illustrations for advertisements, catalog covers and illustrations, and kindred work. On many occasions a commercial illustrator is required to make a drawing for a bird's-eye view of the grounds of some manufacturing plant, or a catalog illustration showing a technical device or piece of apparatus in perspective. The method of laying out and finishing the drawing, etc. depends on the kind of drawing being made and on the individual tricks devised by the particular artist working on the drawing, or the customs of the particular art department. In all cases, however, the artist must understand the rules of perspective.

11. Bird's-eye views are simply perspective views with the horizon very high, as if viewed by the observer from the top of a high building or a balloon, or as viewed by the eye of a bird hundreds of feet above the ground. whence the name *bird's-eye view.* Frequently, the illustrator is called upon to make a bird's-eye view of a group of factory buildings, or

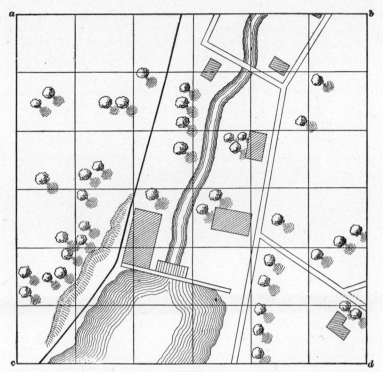

Fig. 3

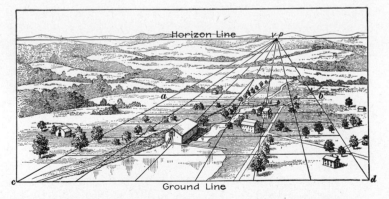

Horizon Line

v p

a

b

c

d

Ground Line

Fig. 4

similar scene, for use in a catalog or prospectus, or on the
billheads, letter paper, and envelopes of the firm.

Generally, no photograph or drawing can be made direct
from the scene, because there is no elevated point from which
such photograph or drawing can be made, and besides, such
a view is sometimes asked for before the buildings are constructed. The artist therefore has nothing to work from except
a plan showing the location of buildings, trees, fields, fences,
streams, etc., in the scene. This plan is absolutely necessary
in order to get the correct relative positions of the various
buildings, trees, fields, streams, etc., and can be obtained,
usually drawn to a definite scale, from the people for whom
the work is being done.

12. Let it be supposed that Fig. 3 is such a plan and
that it has been lightly ruled with squares, as shown. When
a bird's-eye view is then being made, it is a simple matter to
establish the horizon well up in the picture and, at a convenient distance below (say 100 feet to scale), to place the ground
line. Then the actual length $c\,d$, from the plan or map in
Fig. 3, is laid off on the ground line, as $c\,d$, Fig. 4, and then
the network of squares is laid out in perspective, as at a, b, c, d,
Fig. 4, thus determining the positions of the various buildings, etc. The actual heights of the buildings may be laid
off on vertical measuring lines or plotted in freehand. In
this way the entire bird's-eye view may be plotted pictorially
in outline and then rendered in pen and ink, as in Fig. 4,
or in wash or water colors.

MAKING A PERSPECTIVE DRAWING OF A MECHANICAL DEVICE

13. A very common problem for the commercial artist is the
making of a perspective view of a mechanical device, or some
part thereof, to be used as an illustration in a catalog or for a
technical article. While in many cases a photograph of the
device will serve the purpose just as well, frequently a perspective view (properly rendered) is required before the device
has been constructed so as to show just how the device will
look and work when actually made up.

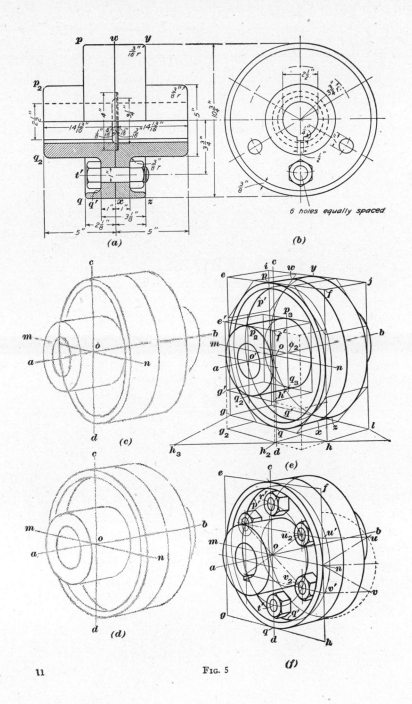

6 holes equally spaced

(a)

(b)

(c)

(d)

(e)

(f)

11

FIG. 5

In this case all that will be furnished the pictorial artist will be a side-view drawing that shows the device partly in section and a full-front elevation drawing. From these two views, which are usually in blueprint form, the artist must construct a perspective view and later render it so that it will look like the finished article. Unless he can do this he will be seriously handicapped in his work as a commercial artist. Such work must not be considered as mechanical drawing; the pictorial artist has nothing to do with the designing of the device or the making of the side and elevation views, as these views are handed to him in complete form.

14. The procedure followed in making such a perspective drawing of a mechanical device is shown in Fig. 5 (a) to (f). In (a) is shown a side view, partly in section, and at (b) a full-front elevation of what is known in mechanics as a flange coupling used to connect two lengths of shafting. The upper half of the side view (a) shows the outside of the coupling, and the lower half shows the appearance of the coupling as it would be if it were cut through halfway up vertically. The shaded parts indicate that portion that would be solid metal, and the unshaded portions (in lower half of the view only) represent the sunken and the hollow parts. The nuts are shown in side view.

15. First Stage.—Before the perspective diagram is drawn, a rough, freehand, trial, pencil sketch must be made to determine at about what angle the device must be placed in order to show the sunken surface where the six nuts are placed. This sketch is shown in (c); but while a perspective view drawn at such an angle will show the main outside parts of the coupling it will not show the sunken portion of the face in such a way that the nuts can be properly portrayed. It is evident, therefore, that the view must show the front of the coupling swung around more toward the face of the observer.

16. Second Stage.—A second, rough, freehand, pencil sketch, view (d), is next made with the front showing more than in the first sketch. The amount of projection of the hub, or portion that fits over the shaft and which resembles the end of a gun barrel, as well as the amount of depression of the sunken face, the thickness of the flanges, etc. can all be obtained from view (a); the vertical and other dimensions can be obtained from view (b).

These two trial sketches are based, first, on the main vanishing line, or axis, a b, and second on the vertical axis c d which will represent the face plane of the large circle of the flange. The vanishing line, or axis, a b may be considered as vanishing at V P (Right), but the commercial artist need not bother to letter vanishing points as long as he knows where they are located.

17. Third Stage.—When the general angle at which the coupling should be drawn has been determined, the accurate perspective drawing should be made. This may be done by first drawing a rectangular box in perspective and then drawing within this the main, or wheel, portion of the coupling.

To draw this box, lay out the general vanishing line, or the axis, a b, at the same vanishing angle as in view (d). Then obtain, from view (a), the diameter p q of the largest circle and lay it out as the vertical line f h in view (e). This line may be considered as being in contact with the picture plane and upon it all vertical measurements are laid off and projected backwards to their proper places. Lay off vanishing lines e f and g h, vanishing them to an imaginary point V P (Left). If great accuracy is required, measuring points may be located and the actual width of the box laid out on the horizontal measuring line h h_3 and then projected toward the imaginary measuring point M P (Left). The intersection of this line with the vanishing line g h is the position of the point g. The erection of the vertical g e completes the rectangle e f h g. The perspective rectangle to form the rear of the box is found in the same way after the thickness of the box, q z, view (a), has been laid out on the horizontal measuring line in view (e), projected back to form the perspective depth h l.

In practice, however, these retreating distances, especially such small ones as h l, will be plotted in by eye measurement.

Having completed the perspective box, its corners can be cut off as shown, thus making an octagonal box, in which it will be a simple matter to draw ellipses.

18. First the front great circle $p\,q$ should be sketched in as an ellipse, then the rear great circle $y\,z$, the two ellipses being connected by retreating horizontal lines $p\,y$ and $q\,z$. Then the smaller of the two front great circles should be sketched as an ellipse, about $\frac{1}{8}$ inch within front ellipse $p\,q$. The next step is to sketch in another ellipse $p'\,q'$ a distance back of the face plane $e\,f\,h\,g$ equal to a little less than one-third of $h\,l$, the thickness of the box. This represents the face of the depressed portion of the flange, on which are the nuts and from which the hub emerges. Of course only the left half of this depressed ellipse will show in the finished perspective drawing, but its entire form must be drawn in the pencil sketch.

19. Next the hub of the coupling must be drawn, which is done as follows: The actual amount that the hub projects in front of the face plane is obtained from view (a), namely, the distance between vertical lines $p\,q$ and $p_2\,q_2$, and may be laid off freehand on horizontal line $h_3\,h$, at h_2. From point h_2 a line is then vanished back toward $V\,P$ (*Left*) and marked $h_2\,g_2$; the length of this line is the diameter of the face of the hub taken from view (b), and is estimated by eye measurement. In this way the perspective rectangle $e'\,f'\,g'\,h'$ can be formed, the perspective height of the rectangle also being estimated freehand. Within this rectangle may be drawn the two ellipses showing the face of the hub. The ellipse $p_3\,q_3$ is then drawn to show where the hub joins the depressed face of the main, or wheel, portion of the coupling, by first laying off point o_2 on the retreating axis $a\,b$ a distance (in perspective) back of o equal to the amount of depression back of face plane $e\,f\,h\,g$, which is found by reference to view (a). The vertical axis $p_3\,q_3$ is then drawn and the ellipse sketched in to meet the retreating lines $p_2\,p_3$ and $q_2\,q_3$. It remains only to sketch in the great ellipse $w\,x$, midway between great ellipses $p\,q$ and $y\,z$, and the main portions of the outline perspective coupling are completed.

20. Fourth Stage.—The fourth and last stage of making such an outline perspective drawing is shown in view (f), where the six nuts are put in perspective. In this view most of the construction lines and reference letters of view (e) are omitted, so that the perspective drawing of the nuts can be more clearly shown.

These nuts rest against the depressed face of the coupling, represented by ellipse $p_1 q_1$, and their faces are practically level with the face plane $e f g h$. As the center of the face of each nut falls on a large circle, the diameter of this circle is taken from view (b) and laid off on the vertical measuring line $f h$ in view (f). A dotted semicircle is then drawn to the right of this vertical and divided into thirds at points u and v. If a line is vanished back from the top of the dotted semicircle to $V P$ $(Left)$, the point where it cuts vertical center line $c d$, point r', will be the center of the top nut. Similarly, a line vanished back from the bottom of the dotted semicircle will locate point t' as the center of the bottom nut. A line projected over from point u to u' on the vertical measuring line $f h$, and then vanished back until it cuts ellipse $r' t'$ on the right-hand curve will locate the center of the upper right-hand nut at u_2. The upper left-hand nut is found by continuing the vanishing line back from u' until it cuts the left-hand portion of the ellipse $r' t'$. The lower right-hand and left-hand nuts are located in the same way by vanishing a line back from v'.

21. Having located the centers of the nuts, little hexagons, the dimensions of which can be secured from view (b), are laid off around these centers and small ellipses drawn within them as shown. The half-rounded faces of the nuts may be drawn freehand, which will give each hexagonal side a convex formation, which must be drawn in freehand. The depth of the nuts is determined by the limits of the depressed face, and is obtained, as in the case of view (e), from point o to o_2. This completes the outline perspective drawing of this mechanical device. Before it is a finished illustration, however, it must be rendered, preferably by means of the air brush.

completed the rear corner and the adjacent sides. This gave him a box corner in which to build up his scene. It was then a simple matter to draw vertical *g h*, the nearest corner of the jury box, and vanish the lines from *g* and *h* (and points between them) toward *V P* (*Left*), for the left side of the jury box [because that side is parallel with the right-hand wall, which vanishes at *V P* (*Left*)], and to vanish lines *g i* and *h j* toward *V P* (*Right*) as shown, because this front part of the jury box is parallel with the left-hand wall, which vanishes at *V P* (*Right*). Line *k l*, and other lines of the desk along the right-hand wall, vanish at *V P* (*Left*) as does the right-hand wall. The verticals *s t*, *u v*, *o p*, *q r*, and *m n*, assist in locating window niche, abutment, etc. as shown. With the details of the room thus placed the figures can be arranged accurately in their proper positions.

It should be noticed that the figures at the lower right-hand corner are quite large, because they were very near the artist who was making the sketch. Further, as the figures recede to the rear corner they grow very much smaller.

PERSPECTIVE IN CARTOON WORK

24. Application of Perspective to Cartoons.—As a cartoon is a composition illustration that carries a message and points a moral, it is absolutely necessary for the cartoonist to be familiar with perspective. Cartoons, even those in series, but especially those of the higher class, constantly require accessories of trees, roads, streets, houses, furniture, etc., all of which must be drawn with accuracy. To the art student preparing to do cartooning and caricaturing, perspective is, therefore, of as great importance as to any other class of illustrator.

25. The cartoon in Fig. 8 well shows the necessity for the cartoonist to understand perspective. In this case the artist desired to convey the idea that the man who skilfully rolls the ball shown can knock down every time those particular pins and thus make a "strike" in his personal progress.

The cartoonist could have drawn the bowling alley as if viewed from the side and make the man bowling (at one end) and the knocked-down pins (at the other end) of equal prominence. This, however, would not have conveyed the thought with sufficient force. The best arrangement is that shown in the picture, where the observer is near the knocked-down pins (which are the largest things in the picture) and is looking back up the alleys toward the bowlers and the racks for the balls.

Not only is perspective shown by the vanishing lines of the boards of the alleys, but also by the small size of the figures of the bowlers at the other end of the alleys. It is easily seen that the picture was laid out in parallel perspective; the eyes of the distant figures made on a level with the eyes of the observer, and all the details sketched in and rendered freehand.

PERSPECTIVE IN MAGAZINE AND BOOK ILLUSTRATING

26. Application of Perspective to Fiction and Other High-Class Illustration.—It is frequently thought that, the farther away one gets from mechanical, architectural, or diagrammatic drawings, and the nearer he approaches high-grade fiction and like illustrations, the less a knowledge of perspective is needed. However, the reverse is the case.

The illustrator cannot compose pictures "out of his head," he must have sketches of exterior or interior views or objects that may be used in, or adapted to the pictorial work that he is doing. Therefore, in composing the general setting of a picture, he follows first the laws and methods of freehand perspective used in nature sketching.

27. Determining Perspective Angle and Horizon. It is evident that, in a picture or a piece of pictorial decorative work, one cannot place the horizon line, perspective angle, and other points, arbitrarily, as would be the case in a perspective diagram. The conditions in each case must decide just how these elements are to be placed. It is well known that when the horizon is placed low more importance is given to the figures in the composition than when it is placed high. This is because the horizon line is known to be at the observer's eye level, and if the heads and eyes of figures in the picture are above the horizon, they appear taller and more important. Old-time portrait painters (Gainsborough, notably) employed this means of giving importance to their subjects; and in modern times, the poster artist, portrayer of men's fashions, and other commercial advertising artists, use the same trick, sometimes making the soles of the shoes of the figures on a straight line with the observer's eye level.

28. If the picture shows an outdoor scene viewed from a slight hill or eminence, as looking down on a river or lake from a high bank, the horizon will be high. If the picture is an indoor scene, the horizon will not be higher than the eye level of a standing figure. . But it may be as low as the eye level of a seated figure. This is illustrated in Figs. 6 and 7, where the horizon is on a level with the eyes of the newspaper artist who sketched it, as he was seated on a chair.

29. When determining the most suitable angle of perspective to use, a safe rule to follow is to use angular perspective for interior views, if much of the room is to be shown, and either parallel or angular perspective for exterior views. This rule, however, is not an arbitrary one. If parallel perspective is used for interior views, where much of the room is shown, the rear end of the room will appear as a rectangle within the rectangle of the picture's outline, from the corners of which lines run out sharply to the border lines. Angular perspective (not necessarily 45° perspective) presents no such objections. In all cases the vanishing lines should be clothed with details and accessories to the picture so that no unbroken straight lines and sharp angles will appear and thus spoil the harmony of good composition.

30. Placing of Figures.—The most important point to remember when placing human figures in a composition is that not only the eye of the observer, but also the eyes

of all standing figures in the scene or picture, correspond with
the level of the horizon line. This is illustrated in Fig. 9.
The observer or the one who is drawing the picture, is supposed
to be standing; therefore the nearest figure, the one at the
left of the picture, is drawn with her eyes level with the horizon
line and the bottom of her skirt say 5 feet below the horizon
line. Assuming that the other two figures are in a direct

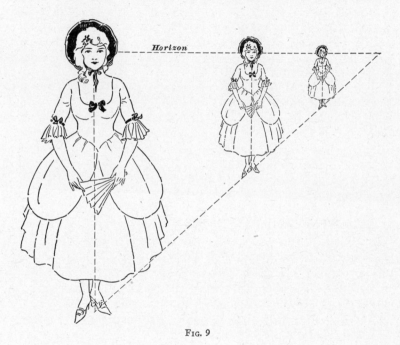

Fig. 9

line extending backwards into the distance, all that is necessary is to draw a line from the lower part of the skirt of the
nearest figure back to the vanishing point $V P$ [$V P$ (Right)
or whatever it may be]. The eyes of these two distant figures
are of course on the horizon, and thus their heights are determined. While the figures will decrease in height the farther
they are from the observer, this decrease in height always
occurs at the foot, for the head remains on the same level

because the eyes of all adult figures of the same height, standing on the same horizontal plane (as the ground, a floor, etc.), must always be on the horizon line.

31. Of course, if a standing figure of smaller size than the average adult is used in a composition, or if a child, or dog, for instance, accompanies the standing adult figure, the eye level of the child will be very much below the eye level of the adult. For instance, the eye level of a 9- or 10-year old child may be about 4 or $4\frac{1}{2}$ feet above the ground. In sketching such a child in relation to the adult figure in the composition, the proper height should be marked off somewhere on the nearest standing adult figure (say at a level with armpit or shoulder), a short horizontal line projected over to right or left, and the child sketched in. To indicate the positions of other children in the picture, lines from the head and the feet of the nearest child are vanished back toward $V P$, and thus the apparent heights of other children in the picture are determined.

32. If the figures were not all on a straight vanishing line, for example, if the middle figure, in Fig. 9, were somewhere to the right of its present position but just as far back, the procedure would be just as simple. The dotted vanishing line for the feet of the figures would be drawn as before, then a horizontal line drawn from the position where the middle figure now is to the point to the right where the second figure would then be standing. This point then obtained would be the feet, or bottom of the skirt, of the figure, but her eyes would be on the horizon as before.

33. If the observer is seated, and all the figures in the picture are seated, the horizon line should pass uniformly through their eyes as before. If the observer is seated and some of the figures in the picture standing, the eyes of the standing figures will of course be some 15 or 20 inches (to scale) above the horizon line. This principle was illustrated in Figs. 6 and 7.

I L T 22—9

Drawn by F. C. Yohn

FIG. 10   22

e
f
g
h
UVP
n
m
i
j
VP
Horizon Line
a   Ground Line   b

Fig. 11

34. In Fig. 10 is shown a high-grade fiction illustration
in which, at first, it may seem that perspective has no place;
but a careful study will show that both linear and aerial
perspective are used. Fig. 11 shows how the tents are accurately vanished toward UVP, because they are on the slope
of a slight hill and therefore vanish upwards in oblique parallel
perspective. The horizon line passes through the eye level
of the large figure in the foreground, but the eyes of the three
marching figures in the middle distance are above the horizon,
because these figures are partly on the hill, and not down to
the level of the soldier in the foreground.

35. To determine the height and position of these distant
figures, ground line $a\,b$ is extended over to the left, outside
the limits of the diagram in Fig. 11, and a point (which could
be called x, although not seen) is selected on this ground line
sufficiently far to the left of the large soldier in the foreground
to indicate how far to the left in the picture are these marching
soldiers. From this point, a line is vanished back and up
to $U\,V\,P$; the only part of this vanishing line that shows
in the picture is line $j\ U\,V\,P$. Upon vanishing line $j\ U\,V\,P$,
point m locates the feet of the marching soldier.
To find the height of this soldier a line from the top of
the head of the large soldier in the foreground is extended
over to the left (outside the limits of the diagram in Fig. 11),
and where it meets a vertical erected at point x (outside the
limits of the diagram) could be called point y (although not
seen in the diagram). Vertical $x\,y$ will then be the height of
the large soldier in the foreground, although to the extreme
left. From the top of this vertical (unseen point y) a line
will then be vanished back and up to $U\,V\,P$, although this
vanishing line is not marked on the diagram. Where the
vertical erected at m and extended upwards cuts the vanishing
line just described will locate point n; $m\,n$ therefore is the
height of the distant marching soldier.

36. In a similar manner vanishing lines $i\ U\,V\,P$ and
$h\ U\,V\,P$ will locate the feet and head of one of the other distant
marching soldiers. The locations and heights of the distant

tents or huts are found in a similar manner. Vanishing lines from e, f, g, and h to $U V P$ locate the heights, and vanishing lines from i and j to $U V P$ give the slope of the descending ground plane down which the soldiers are marching.

37. Aerial perspective is well shown in Fig. 10 by using dark crisp values on the clothing of the soldier in the foreground, making the clothing of the marching soldiers not so dark and distinct, and the values of the tents very faint and light.

Other pictures should be studied and analyzed, with a view to determining how linear and aerial perspective are used therein, just as has been done with the illustrations shown in this Section. Ample opportunity will be given, in connection with the next section (devoted to pictorial composition), to study and analyze numerous examples of practical illustrations in which perspective is used.

38. Perspective of Curves.—In Fig. 12 is reproduced a high-grade magazine illustration, in which the necessity for a thorough knowledge of perspective is evident. It must be remembered that this is not an architectural drawing, but a pictorial sketch by an artist to serve as an illustration. A study of this picture will reveal that the illustrator was not only familiar with the principles of parallel perspective, but also understood and applied the principles of drawing vertical circles in perspective. An attempt to make the drawing for such an illustration as this without a training in perspective would have resulted in failure.

39. In Fig. 13 is shown how the artist first located the horizon line, then the vanishing point $V P$, the retreating lines of ceiling and floor from a, b, c, j, and l toward $V P$, lines from d, e, and f toward $V P$ to determine the upper and the lower limits of the semicircular arches, from f, g, and h to determine the capitals of the columns, and from i and j to locate the bases of these columns. These vanishing lines give the general directions in which all parts vanish.

Vertical lines *r p*, *q o*, *s t*, *u v*, *w x*, *y z*, etc. are then drawn to indicate how the columns are spaced. The widths between

FIG. 12

the columns decrease on a regular ratio, but the pictorial artist trained in perspective can sketch in these widths by eye measurement. The upper parts of these vertical lines, being crossed by horizontal retreating lines $d\,V\,P$ and $f\,V\,P$,

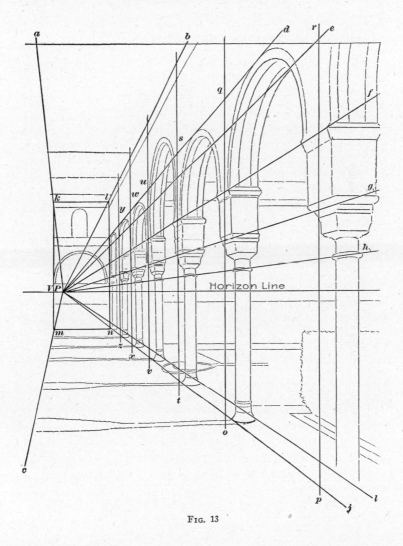

Fig. 13

form rectangles in perspective in which semiellipses may be sketched in freehand as shown. The rectangle k, l, n, m at

the far end of the cloister may then be sketched in as shown,
and the drawing then rendered in pen and ink or other medium.

PERSPECTIVE IN INTERIOR DECORATION

40. Application of Perspective to Interior Decoration Sketches.—Although the training that is being given in perspective is intended for application solely to pictorial work, occasions will arise when the illustrator may be called on to make sketches for interior-decoration schemes. This does not necessarily mean that he must be a decorative designer; as a matter of fact, many pictorial artists who lay out such schemes are not designers but are simply accomplished perspective illustrators.

The firm of decorators will furnish the pictorial artist with flat plans of wall and ceiling decoration, and also a measured plan of the room or rooms, although sometimes the artist must measure the rooms himself and then adapt to the walls and ceilings a decorative treatment devised for a room of other dimensions. From the data available, the pictorial artist will prepare a pictorial perspective sketch showing how the proposed decorative treatment will look when completed.

41. Obtaining Measurements of Room.—In many cases it will be a simple matter to obtain a blueprint (to scale) of the measured plan of the room from the architect, owner, or decorator. In cases where such a blueprint is not available, the artist may himself measure the room. To do this, he should commence at one corner and measure continuously across the side with a 25- or 50-foot tape, recording each projection or recess as it is reached and noting the width of trim, etc. around windows and doors, where such trim is built in before measurements are taken. This should be done with all sides of the room, and then the ceiling height, size of windows and doors, and height of windows above floor should be measured. A special note should be made of chimney breasts, fireplace openings, bay windows, location of gas and electric fixtures, water supply, etc. A survey of a single

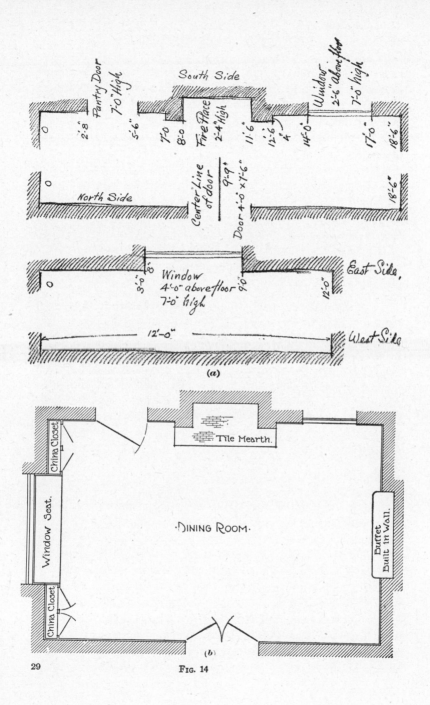

Fig. 14

room after such a system of measurement should be about
as shown in Fig. 14 (a), each side being recorded separately.
All measurements of less than 2 feet should be recorded in
inches (thus, 16″, not 1′ 4″).   Care in the observance of this
rule on all occasions will avoid errors in reading the survey
after it is made.

After all measurements are taken and all information is
recorded, a scale plan of the room should be laid out as in
Fig. 14 (b), and on this plan all the details of the decorative
scheme should be inserted.   Thus, the china closet on each
side of the east window and the buffet built in the west end
of the room are shown, together with the tile hearth in front
of the fireplace.   The side and end walls can then be measured
and laid out in scaled drawings as was the floor plan.

42. Obtaining the Decorative Scheme.—It is not
expected that the pictorial artist shall get up the decorative
scheme for the interior, although it is not impossible that
he should do so.   However, the decorative treatment is usually
submitted as a flat drawing, to scale, either by the decorator
who is going to carry out the work (whether in wallpaper,
frescoing, or woodwork) or by the owner.   Whatever the
decorative scheme, the essential thing is the making of the
perspective drawing and then fitting in the decoration, also
in perspective.

43. Making the Perspective Drawing.—Before actually
laying out the outline perspective drawing, the artist must
decide whether he wants the room to appear in parallel or
in angular perspective, and, if the latter, what angle. Ordinarily,
parallel perspective should be avoided for a decoration sketch;
the result is usually too mechanical and uninteresting unless
the purpose is to show a prominent feature at the opposite
end of a long narrow enclosure, as, for instance, the altar and
chancel of a church, or the large stained-glass memorial window
over the altar or pulpit.   The average interior-decoration
sketch, however should be made in angular perspective, not
necessarily 45° perspective, but perhaps 60° and 30°, 75° and 15°,
etc.   In this way, not only can the most prominent details

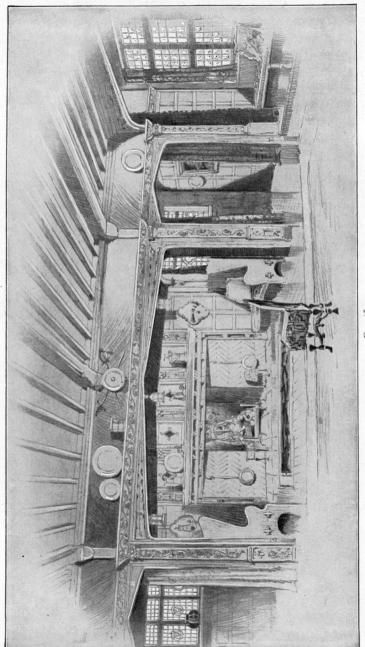

FIG. 15

31

of one wall be clearly shown but details of the adjoining wall
and the ceiling can also be shown.

44.   Such an interior-decoration sketch fully rendered, is
shown in Fig. 15.   The end wall, showing a window seat, makes
an angle of 75° or 80°, while the other wall, showing grate,
mantel, seats, hearth, etc., makes an angle of 15° or 10°.   Not
only the evidences of a careful perspective layout are noticeable
here, but the snap of the rendering, showing black and white
values, cleverly cast shadows and their rendering, and well-
lighted walls so that the decorative details may be clearly seen,
should be given close study.

It is understood, of course, that, when once the panels,
or other wall spaces, in which the decoration is to be placed
have been carefully laid out in perspective, the decorative details
themselves can be drawn in freehand.

PICTORIAL PERSPECTIVE EXERCISES

GENERAL INFORMATION

45.   Required Work in Pictorial Perspective.—As in
the case of the preceding Sections, the final test as to whether
or not the principles and practice of applying the rules of perspective to pictorial work are understood is shown only by the
actual preparation of pictorial work in which perspective
appears.   Therefore, although later an extended training is
given in the actual preparation of composition pictures, an
introductory training in composition is here given by the preparation of simple pictorial perspectives.

This work, as before, will consist of exercises arranged as
two plates, each 15 in. × 20 in., which is the regular full
size sheet of drawing paper.   The plates are to be sent to the
Schools for inspection, as previously described.

**46.   Preliminary Practice Work (Not to Be Sent
In).**—Before starting the work on Plate 1 it will be well to
do the following preliminary practice work on pictorial per-

spective. On a sheet of white paper of the usual size arranged vertically make a pencil sketch direct from nature following the method of working described in this subject. If more convenient, the sketch may be made on the page of a sketch book, not smaller than 8 in. × 10 in., or 6 in. × 8 in., and then pasted on the drawing sheet.

The sketch should be that of a city or town street or a country road, along which are shown houses, trees, etc., getting smaller as they recede into the distance. Do not sketch a landscape in which the location of foreground and background details is vague and uncertain, but make an accurate sketch as described.

On a similar sheet arranged vertically prepare a perspective drawing, in very accurate pencil outline, of a piece of apparatus or a mechanical device. This drawing is to be made in four progressive stages, such as shown in Fig. 5 (c), (d), (e), and (f); namely, the rough trial sketch, the revised trial layout, (if necessary), the accurate diagrammatic skeleton of perspective lines, and the final pencil drawing showing in outline the complete perspective of the device, with the construction lines omitted.

Because of the peculiar nature of the problem, the student is given the option of making the same drawings (larger) shown in Fig. 5 (c), (d), (e), and (f), or of making a perspective layout of an entirely different piece of apparatus, of which he is able to obtain the blueprints or sectional drawings. In the former case, he may proceed in accordance with the text directions accompanying Fig. 5, and work from the illustration. If he is going to draw a different device, he should obtain the sectional drawings, and make drawings for the four progressive stages. By vertical and horizontal center lines the plate should be divided into four, $5\frac{1}{2}'' \times 7\frac{1}{2}''$ rectangles, and each stage drawing should be made about twice the size (four times the area) of those shown in Fig. 5. All drawings (particularly the fourth) must be laid out with the greatest accuracy.

It must be understood, as directed for previous subjects, that none of this preliminary practice work is to be sent in to the Schools. Only numbered drawing plates are to be sent in.

47. Character of Drawing Plates.—The two plates are to comprise original drawings, prepared according to directions given, of a bird's-eye view, and a magazine or book illustration, in the order mentioned. Each one is to be carefully drawn in accordance with the rules of perspective and then rendered in the medium that seems most appropriate.

PLATE 1

48. Perspective Bird's-Eye View.—On the sheet arranged vertically prepare the plan for, and the actual rendering of, a bird's-eye view similar to (but not a copy of) Figs. 3 and 4. The plan, with ruled squares properly arranged should occupy the upper part of the sheet and the rendered bird's-eye view of the lower part.

The plan, or layout for the positions of the buildings, can be roughly sketched in, on large squares, from the known locations of the buildings of a manufacturing plant, groups of buildings on a college campus, a dairy farm, or other groups of buildings, trees, fences, etc. The selected group should be actual buildings in the student's own city or town. The perspective, or bird's-eye view, can then be laid out and rendered as previously described. The rendering can be made in pen-and-ink, wash, or water colors, as preferred.

49. Final Work on Plate 1.—Letter or write the title, Plate 1: Pictorial Perspective, at the top of the sheet, and on the back, in the lower left-hand corner, place class letters and number, name, address, and the date of completing the plate. Roll the plate, place in the mailing tube, and send to the Schools for inspection. If all required redrawn work on previous plates has been completed, proceed with Plate 2.

PLATE 2

50. Perspective Magazine Illustration.—On the sheet arranged vertically make an original composition drawing in perspective of the interior of a business office to serve as the basis, or scene, for an illustration, arranging it so that it shows one corner of a room in angular perspective (60° and 30°).

When the skeleton outline of the interior has been constructed, clothe this outline by portraying rugs, pictures, furniture, etc., in the room. Place two human figures, one seated at a desk and the other entering a door, in the picture in their proper relations to the horizon line, floor, etc. When completed this drawing is not to look like a diagram, but like a finished picture, carefully and thoroughly rendered (not hastily dashed off). Retreating lines, or other straight lines (vertical or horizontal) in the picture, should be partly broken at places by covering or overlapping them with other details in this picture, as by an extending portion of a desk or chair, or the arm or head of one of the figures.

The picture should be rendered with the greatest care in soft pencil, pen and ink, wash, or water color, every effort being exerted to make it a finished illustration suitable for a magazine or book illustration.

51. Final Work on Plate 2.—Letter or write the title, Plate 2: Pictorial Perspective, at the top of the sheet, and on the back, in the lower left-hand corner, place class letters and number, name, address, and the date of completing the plate. Roll the plate, place in the mailing tube, and send to the Schools for inspection.

If any redrawn or rerendered work on either of the plates of this subject has been called for and has not yet been completed, it should be satisfactorily finished at this time. When all required work on the plates of this subject has been completed, the work of the next subject should be taken up at once.

PICTORIAL COMPOSITION

An example of a good pictorial composition
using a group of figures.

PICTORIAL COMPOSITION

Serial 1730 ——— Edition 2

INTRODUCTION

1. Purpose.—The instruction so far has been merely the preliminary training necessary to the actual making of pictures. It has given manual dexterity and skill in drawing all kinds of objects and the handling of the various mediums. It has also made clear the rules and principles that underlie the drawing of parts of a picture in their proper proportions, relations, and relative distances. But it was not intended that these drawings, however well they have been made, should be considered as pictures.

2. Distinction Between a Picture and a Drawing. A **picture** is something that conveys a definite message by means of lines, tones, and colors. A **drawing** does not necessarily convey a message; its purpose may be simply to develop dexterity in draftsmanship. A picture must be a drawing, but a drawing is not always a picture. Art patrons and users of commercial art work buy drawings only because of their pictorial quality, their suitability for some definite purpose, or the message they convey; they do not buy them simply for the draftsmanship displayed therein. The practical illustrator, therefore, does not consider a mere drawing or a study as a picture, nor does he try to sell it as such. It is important that the beginner should understand this fact, for there is a tendency with beginners to attempt to sell drawings that are not made for any definite purpose. Such attempts usually result in disappointment.

Illustrative and decorative work, all coming under the general term, pictures, can be satisfactorily made only when

the principles of pictorial composition are intelligently understood and applied. In the following explanation of these
principles, examples of good pictorial compositions are shown
and described, and suggestions are made for the application of
these principles to pictorial work.

COMPOSITION IN PICTORIAL WORK

ELEMENTS OF COMPOSITION

DEFINITIONS

3. **Composition** is the orderly and harmonious grouping
and arranging of lines and masses so that they will present a
pleasing relation one to another.   Unless the various parts of a
design or picture are so arranged, they are simply isolated parts
and have nothing of interest or value.   For instance, if six
matches or toothpicks are allowed to fall upon a sheet of paper,
the effect, shown in Fig. 1 (*a*), will not be orderly and harmonious and therefore no pleasing arrangement will be formed.   But
if the sticks are purposely arranged as in (*b*), a hexagon will be
formed.   Placing one end of each stick against one end of all
the others and spreading the bodies of the sticks out fanwise,
as in (*c*), produces a sunburst.   Placing them as in (*d*) forms a
six-pointed star.   Still other orderly and harmonious arrangements could be made with the six matches, all illustrating
composition.

Composition, however, also depends on the relative sizes
and shapes of the outlined spaces; the relative tone values,
sizes, and shapes of the masses of black, gray, and white; and
the relative color values, as well as their light and dark values,
and the sizes and shapes of the masses of colors.

4.   Chief Elements.—The chief elements of composition
are *unity, balance, rhythm, harmony,* and *concentration of interest.*
Unity is the holding together of the parts.   **Balance** is the

placing of each part in its proper position so that no part will be unduly emphasized. **Rhythm** is the constant relation and orderly connection of parts. **Harmony** is the consistent arrangement of parts that have something in common, such as size, etc.

In the composition of pictures, however, the parts must also be so arranged as to keep the observer's interest concentrated on the proper object or figure. Unless this is done, the picture will not convey the message or tell the story in the most graphic

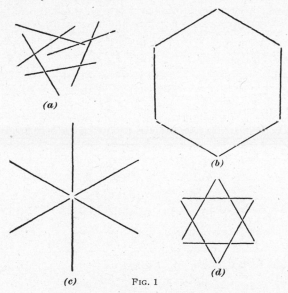

(a)

(b)

(c)   Fig. 1   *(d)*

manner. This **concentration of interest** is accomplished not only by the proper placing of the figures or objects but also by the relative detailing in the rendering.

5. Subelements.—Certain elements, or subelements, of general composition, as related to lines and masses, have not been referred to by name in the foregoing; among these are *principality, opposition, symmetry, order, simplicity, breadth,* and *repose.* But the chief elements, unity, balance, rhythm, harmony, and concentration of interest include and cover the subelements named; so that, when symmetry and order, for instance, are mentioned, it can be well understood that they are various phases of balance. For this reason only the chief elements, unity, balance, rhythm, harmony, and concentration of interest will be discussed.

6. In a composition, it is necessary to have unity of lines and unity of shapes and masses. Unity of lines is obtained when the lines are so arranged that one cannot be changed in any way without affecting the entire composition. When this unity is obtained, the lines are no longer separate elements but are the units of a design. This is illustrated in Fig. 1. In the haphazard arrangement of matches in (a), they bear no relation to one another; they are disconnected and scattered; therefore, the arrangement has no unity. But when grouped as in (b), (c), and (d), they express uniform ideas from which not one of them can be removed without leaving a feeling of incompleteness; therefore, unity is shown. The same necessity for unity exists when the component parts of a composition are outlined shapes, or masses of black and gray or colors.

7. Principle of Mechanical Balance.—Unlimited combinations of lines, shapes, or masses, all of which express unity, can be made but some of them will be more pleasing than others. Whether or not a combination is pleasing depends on the care with which the lines, shapes, or masses have been

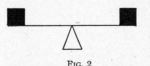

arranged so that each will keep its proper place without being unduly emphasized. The balancing of outlined spaces, or of tone or color masses,

FIG. 2

is subject to the laws that govern the balancing of physical weights. For instance, when a board is balanced evenly over a sawhorse, its center must be over the center of support; and if a weight is placed on one end of the board, to maintain a balance an equal weight must be placed on the other end, as shown in Fig. 2.

The nearer one weight is brought toward the balancing point (the point of support) of the board, the heavier it must be to maintain the balance; and the farther it is removed from the point of support the lighter it becomes. Thus, a weight of 100 pounds placed half way between the end of the

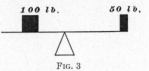

FIG. 3

board and the point of support can be balanced by a weight of 50 pounds placed on the extreme other end, as shown in Fig. 3.

8. **Application of Mechanical Balance to a Composition.**—Applying this principle to the balancing of outlined shapes and tone masses in a drawing, it is found that the two black masses in Fig. 4 (*a*) and (*b*) balance each other perfectly because they are of equal size and weight, and are the same distance from the center (corresponding to the point of support). If one of these spots is gray or white, the two will not balance in the positions shown in Fig. 4 (*a*) and (*b*) because the gray or white spot will be lighter in tone value and, to balance the black one, must be increased in size. This is shown in Fig. 5, where the gray spot *a* is twice the size of the black spot *b*, but its light-and-shade value is only one-half as strong (heavy) as that of *b*, and therefore these two are perfectly balanced when their centers are equidistant from center *c*.

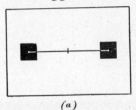

(*a*)

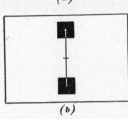

(*b*)

FIG. 4

In Fig. 6 the lighter value *a* is balanced by the darker (heavier) value *b*, although *b* is only one-fourth as large as *a*. Being one-fourth the size and twice the strength (weight) in tone

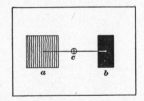

FIG. 5

value, *b* has one-half the value of *a*, and balances with *a* when its center is placed from *c* a distance twice as great as the center of a is placed from c.   In general these same principles apply to the balance of black and white values and to the balance of gray and white values.

9.   Securing Pleasing Balance in a Composition.—In Fig. 7, (a) to (f), are shown line arrangements expressing both unity and balance and therefore of varied interest.   The square in (a), divided by the vertical line, shows an exact symmetrical balance of the two rectangular spaces, just as an exact symmetrical balance is shown in the diagrams in Figs. 2 and 4 (a). The square in (b), crossed by vertical and horizontal center lines, also shows exact symmetrical balance, just as exact symmetrical balance is shown in Figs. 2 and 4 (b).

In Fig. 7 (c) is shown vertically, and in (d) horizontally, the balance of outlined spaces on the principles of mechanical

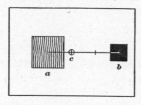

FIG. 6

balance shown in Figs. 3, 5, and 6. Such balance is also shown in Fig. 7 (e), where vertical and horizontal lines and spaces are combined.   In (f), the principle of proper proportion of outlined spaces in a square or a rectangle is shown, experience showing that the most pleasing division is to assign three vertical parts to the upper space and five vertical parts to the lower space.

10.   The arrangements in Fig. 8, (a) to (f), illustrate balance of tone masses based on the figures illustrating balance of outlined masses in Fig. 7 (a) to (f).   In Fig. 8 (a) the two tone masses balance each other exactly and symmetrically because they are of the same size and tone value and are arranged equally on each side of a vertical center line.   In (b), the balance is also exact and symmetrical, vertically and horizontally, because the masses are of the same size and tone value.   However, both (a) and (b), while showing exact balance, are not as interesting as are the remaining examples.   In (c), the narrow black space at the left balances the larger white space and gray space at the center and the right because, though smaller, it is just as dense or heavy.   Similarly, the black space in (d), balances

the spaces at the middle and bottom. In (e), the vertical and
the horizontal arrangements are combined, but still illustrate the
principle of small black masses balancing large gray or large
white masses. In (f), the upper dark mass balances the lower

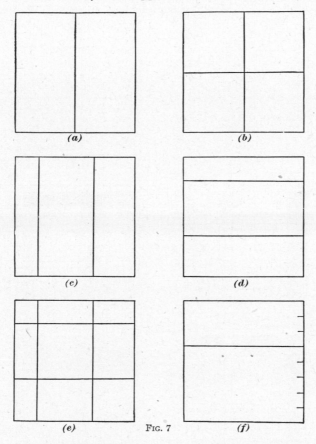

(a)   (b)

(c)   (d)

(e)   FIG. 7   (f)

gray mass, the actual vertical space relation being about three
to five, as explained for Fig. 7 (f).

11. The diagrams in Fig. 8 (c), (d), (e), and (f) are simply
graphic applications of the mechanical principles of balance of
blacks, grays, and whites shown in Figs. 5 and 6. The student
should plot out for himself other diagrams illustrating these

principles. It should be borne in mind that these abstract graphic diagrams of space and mass balancing are intended to teach the underlying principles of space and mass balancing in a picture.

The masses of white, gray, and black in a picture require careful balancing, no matter what may be their shapes or con-

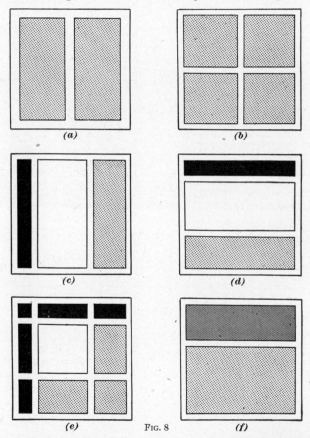

Fig. 8

tours. Sometimes these contours may be very irregular and complicated; and it is therefore necessary to prepare for showing balance of such complicated masses by learning first how to balance masses of more simple shapes. The application to pictorial work will be discussed and illustrated later.

12. Rhythm and Harmony of Lines.—Rhythm is that constant and systematic variation of the relation of the parts or values that gives to the drawing charm and interest and prevents monotony. It may be in the parts or details of the drawing or in the tone values.

In Fig. 9 (a), nine vertical lines are shown within the rectangle, all the same length and the same distance apart. While in this drawing there is unity and to some degree balance, there is monotony, just as there would be monotony if a pianist would strike the same key nine times in succession. But in (b) the first, third, fourth, sixth, seventh, and ninth strokes are shorter than the second, fifth, and eighth strokes, with the result that strokes are in the following regular order: short, long, short; short, long, short; short, long, short. In (c), the idea is carried still further by making the two short strokes adjoin-

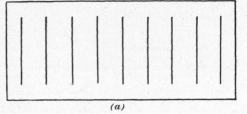

(a)

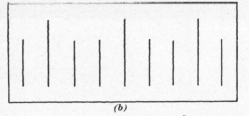

(b)

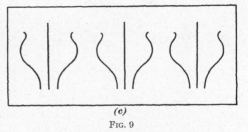

(c)

FIG. 9

ing the long ones symmetrically curved, as shown. Thus, in (b) and (c) is shown related movement; a continuous alternating rise and fall, just as there is a rise and fall of the waves of the sea or tones in a musical composition. The application of this form of rhythm and harmony to pictorial work will be shown later.

13. Another form of rhythm is that in which there is an orderly and consistent changing of relative direction or movement of parts in a drawing. In Fig. 10 (*a*) are shown nine inclined straight lines, none of which have the same direction, and all are so arranged as to present a very confused and disagreeable effect. In (*b*), however, these nine inclined straight lines are arranged so that each succeeding one slants just a little farther from the preceding one than did that one from its predecessor; the whole series thus present a rhythmic movement that is pleasing. In (*c*), the lines are made curved instead of straight and the wavelike effect is made even more pronounced, and thus rhythm is expressed.

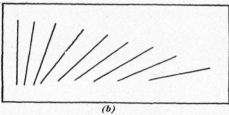

(a)

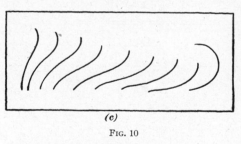

(b)

(c)

Fig. 10

Fig. 11 (*a*) and (*b*) suggest the value of considering the rhythmic arrangement as the foundation for a picture. The sketch in (*a*) may very easily be the basis of a true portrayal of a stream flowing toward the observer around the edge of a hill or mountain, but it lacks grace and rhythm. This is corrected in (*b*), where rhythmic lines are used.

14. Fig. 12 (*a*) and (*b*) illustrates how an establishment of the lines of rhythm in (*a*) enables the entire decorative composition to be drawn with such pleasing effect as shown in (*b*).

This figure also illustrates the association of harmony with rhythm. While in art, the term harmony is usually applied to the proper relation of colors, there is also harmony of line and

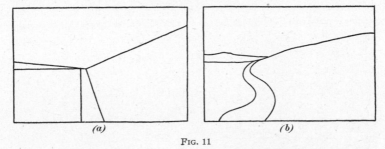

(a) (b)

FIG. 11

mass in composition In this connection harmony means appropriateness or fitness. For instance, in Fig. 12 (b), the two figures and the lines and masses of the scroll and the leaves

(a)   FIG. 12   (b)

fit well within and are perfectly adapted for the shape of the enclosing space. This design, however, would not fit well within a square and there would be a lack of harmony. From this, therefore, it is evident that fitness must be considered when a picture is laid out, in order that harmony may be expressed.

15. Rhythm and Harmony of Tone Values.—Rhythm and harmony apply not only to lines and outline shapes; but

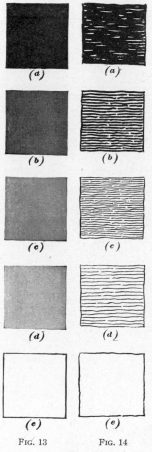

there must also be rhythm of tone values. Just as the eye is carried along in orderly related movement by the proper placing of rhythmic lines, so it can and should be carried along in orderly sequence by the tone values in a composition.

In Fig. 13 are shown five tone values, made from washes, in proper order: (a) black, (b) dark gray, (c) gray, (d) light gray, and (e) white. In Fig. 14 are five tone values, in similar order, made from pen-and-ink drawings. Close inspection will show that the relative differences in tone value between any two adjoining squares are the same. For instance, (c) is just as much lighter than (b) as (b) is lighter than (a). Thus, orderly rhythm or movement of decreasing tone values is expressed.

FIG. 13   FIG. 14

16. Figs. 15 and 16 are examples of lack of rhythm, which is shown by comparing them with Fig. 17, where smooth rhythm of values is expressed. In Fig. 15, the contrast between (b) and (c) is so much greater than between (b) and (a) that there is no rhythm.   There is likewise no rhythm in Fig. 16, because the transition from the tone value of (a) to that of (b) is much more abrupt than from (b) to (c); in other words, (b) is much lighter than (a) though (c) is not much lighter than (b). In Fig. 17, however, rhythm is correctly shown, for (*a*), (*b*), and (*c*) progress evenly in tone value from one to the other, and the step from (*a*) to (*b*) is practically the same as the step from (*b*) to (*c*). It is an even progression that is smooth and satisfactory, giving a feeling of restfulness. Further, comparing these values with those in Fig. 14 shows that the jump from (*b*) to (*c*), Fig. 15, is practically the same as the jump from (*b*) to (*e*), Fig. 14; while in Fig. 16 the jump from (*a*) to (*b*) is practically the same as the jump from (*a*) to (*d*), Fig. 14. In Fig. 17, however, the values (*a*), (*b*), and (*c*) correspond to the val-

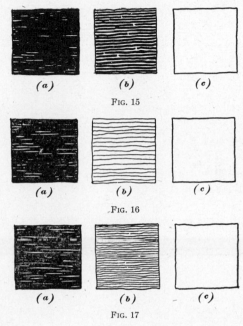

(a)   *(b)*   *(c)*

FIG. 15

(a)   *(b)*   *(c)*

FIG. 16

(a)   *(b)*   *(c)*

FIG. 17

ues (*a*), (*c*), and (*e*) of Fig. 14, and therefore express rhythm. The use of such related values in a picture would give more satisfactory results than the use of unrelated values.

CONCENTRATION OF INTEREST

17. The most important element of composition in pictures is concentration of interest, by which the observer's attention is attracted to and centered upon a certain part of the picture, thus assisting in the graphic portrayal of what the text of the story relates.

The methods by which such concentration of interest is accomplished are best discussed, not as theories, but as practical working plans; these methods will therefore be treated in detail and illustrated when the drawing of the picture is discussed.

PLANNING THE PICTURE

18. **Determining the Idea of the Picture.**—In the application of the theories of composition, it must not be forgotten that in every picture the idea is the thing of greatest importance and that the drawing is secondary to it. Time and effort spent in making, for the purpose of selling, drawings of isolated objects, figures, or landscapes that express no idea and tell no story are simply wasted.

The source of the idea, whether it originates with the artist or is suggested to him by some one else, depends largely on the class of work being done. In newspaper and commercial advertisement work, the main idea is occasionally supplied by the art editor or advertiser, but considerable latitude for the display of originality in carrying out the work is usually allowed the artist. When the pictures are to illustrate a story in a book or magazine, the artist may select the passages he desires to illustrate, or the passages may be designated by the publisher or, in some cases, by the author. But, whatever the source may be, one central idea must be decided on before the actual illustration is begun.

19. **Selecting Objects or Figures for a Picture.** Having decided upon the idea and having made a mental picture of the illustration, which must be as it will afterwards appear on the paper, the artist must look for the material he will need. In doing this, there are a number of things to be looked up.

He should become familiar with the text of the story or article, in order that he may be fully in accord with what is said and so may correctly portray that which is to be illustrated. It is his business to supplement the verbal descriptions so as to make the author's characters and the scenes or articles described appear very realistic. This can be done only when the artist is familiar with the customs and habits of the particular class of people about whom the author is writing. If he has not this familiarity, he should at once become fully acquainted with the local color needed. The correct historical setting for a picture can be obtained by visiting museums and by looking over the illustrations in old magazines and in books.

If the picture is for an advertisement, a familiarity with the merits and selling points of the advertised article should be obtained.

It will also be necessary to get together the careful sketches of the human and animal figures to be used in the picture, both in repose and in action. The posed models from which these studies are made may be friends or acquaintances that will be willing to pose for 15 or 20 minutes at a time, or they may be professional models, if such can be secured. By means of models the artist can get not only the general lines of posture or action needed for the picture, but also the detailed drawing and modeling of the hands, feet, face, drapery, etc. In this connection, one of the most important items of the preliminary memoranda will be sketches or snapshot photographs of action studies. If the picture is to contain figures in action, many quick pencil sketches should be made of persons in such forms of action as one may see on the street every day, and particularly in such postures as will be required for the picture. Snapshot photographs and pictures clipped from magazines and newspapers showing action studies should be collected and preserved in classified form in a scrapbook. The student has already been taught how to prepare these sketches.

20. Necessity for Preliminary Planning.—Most important of all, the student must realize the necessity of actually doing this preliminary planning, securing the data, etc. The common mistake made by beginners in attempting to do creative pictorial work of any kind is to begin a picture, a cartoon, or an advertisement drawing, with nothing before him but the blank paper. Such attempts to evolve pictorial work will always result in failure in the case of the novice. Even professional workers with years of experience use models, preliminary sketches of accessories, etc., in getting up their pictures. The directions as given above must, therefore, be considered as advice as to *what to do,* and not merely descriptive matter to be read and laid aside.

DRAWING THE PICTURE

21. Deciding the Proper Shape and Size.—The shape and size have an important bearing on the success of the picture, and are the first elements that influence composition. These, of course, depend on the use to which the reproduction of the picture is to be put. The shape of a typical full-page illustration for an ordinary octavo size book is considerably different from that of a street-car advertisement picture or the cover of a catalog that opens endwise. The shape and size of an illustration for a story depends entirely on the shape and size of the full page in the book or magazine in which the story is to be published. This information will usually be given to the artist by the publisher or editor when the illustration assignment is made. If not, the illustrator must find out definitely what is wanted and then lay out the drawing with all dimensions enlarged anywhere from one and one-half to three or four times the dimensions of the finished cut. The method of such enlargement and the scale at which it is usually made for various classes of work are discussed elsewhere. The purpose in making the original drawing on such an enlarged scale is to minimize in the finished cut any irregularities of rendering in the original drawing.

22. Determining Main Feature of Picture.—While in mentally planning his picture the illustrator has a general conception of what he wants to draw, he must be more specific when he lays out the preliminary sketches. He must first determine what is to be the most prominent feature, in order to secure the proper concentration of interest.

Usually this feature is one of the persons prominent in the story or feature article, although it may be an object. In some cases the interest may be confined to a single figure; in other cases it may be centered on two or more figures. If the picture is to illustrate an advertisement, the chief thing of interest is the article of merchandise that is sold. If the illustration is a fashion picture, it is the actual gown, hat, or suit that must be given the greatest prominence. First of all, therefore, the artist must so intelligently analyze the situation as to decide what is the most important feature, and must form his mental picture in which he places most prominently this most important object, and in places of less prominence those objects that are of less importance.

23. Applying the Theoretical Principles of Composition.—Before even the preliminary sketches can be made, the principles of composition must be considered. This sometimes necessitates the placing of objects in various positions before the best effects are secured. In this work a cardboard frame with an opening 6 in.×8 in. or 8 in.×10 in. may be advantageously used. When this is held a short distance in front of the eye, it will limit the view and show various tentative arrangements for the composition of the picture.

24. For experimenting in arrangement, certain of the wooden models, such as the vase, cube, sphere, and cone, for instance, may be used. The object now is to secure concentration of interest. Upon first thought, the best arrangement may seem to be the placing of these objects as shown in Fig. 18 (a) and (c), but when viewed through the finder it is found that there is nothing in these arrangements that will cause the attention to be concentrated on some one model. If the frame is removed, there will be no reason to associate the models as a group and they will have no interest in common. These, therefore, are poor arrangements for they lack unity.

In (b), unity and concentration of interest have been secured by placing the cube at one side of the center of the group. The cone is then placed to one side and back of it, so as not to overpower it.

25. Care must be observed that the objects in the picture are not so placed as to violate balance. Although in Fig. 18 (b) and (d) the large cube is really not balanced on the central vertical line of balance, yet in each case the group shows proper balance. In (b) the placing of the cone, and in (d) the placing of the vase and the sphere, establish proper balance of the groups.

26. While, as a unit, the cube and cone in Fig. 18 (*a*) balance perfectly within the rectangle, the effect is not pleasing because there is monotony and stiffness.   When the models are placed as in (*b*), however, balance is maintained.   Besides, interest is added by placing the cone, which has greater apparent volume, slightly to the right of the vertical center line and the cube, which has a less apparent volume, a greater distance to the left of the vertical center line.

To sum up, the most satisfactory and most pleasing pictorial arrangements of objects within a given shape or space will result if, first of all, the principal object is placed somewhere near the center of the picture and the subordinate objects to one side and back of or in front of the principal object, not on a line with it.   The objects should appear to be related by the manner in which they are placed, but should not all occupy the same plane, either vertically front and back, or vertically right and left, but should be so arranged that, if looked down upon from above, their bases in relation to one another will form an irregular figure with closely related points.

27.   Importance of Balance of Tone Masses.—One of the chief considerations that will determine the interest and success of the picture as a graphic illustration, is the correct placing of the tone masses and the color masses when making the drawing; for every picture to be realistic will consist of tones of black and white or of colors.   In order to give true pictorial value to any illustration, therefore, the tone values of the surroundings, background accessories, etc., must be considered, just as are the values of the principal objects, although these tone values are given as much importance as the latter.   For example, the desired emphasis may be given to a light object in the picture by placing it against a dark background; or emphasis may be given to a dark object by placing it against a light or medium-toned background as shown in Fig. 18.

28. Further, the tones of the various parts of the picture and the manner in which they are placed in relation to one another have a great bearing upon the way in which the objects themselves must be placed.   For instance, the cube in Fig. 19,

POOR COMPOSITION   GOOD COMPOSITION

(a)   *(b)*

(c)   *(d)*

Fig. 18

Fig. 19

if drawn simply in outline, the background and foreground spaces being also simply in outline, would appear to be placed very much too far to the left, the background spaces being very much out of proportion, without true balance. However, the strong black value of the cast shadow, combined with the dark values of the shaded side of the cube and of the upper background, compensate for the extreme left-hand placing of the cube, and the eye therefore judges the cube to be properly placed within the outline. If the cube were placed directly on

Fig. 20

the vertical center line of the rectangle, the dark value of the cast shadow combined with that of the shaded side would so greatly overbalance the light values in the left of the rectangle as to disturb balance seriously. Thus the tone values, the masses of dark and light, determine the proper balance of the composition.

29. Importance of Rhythm and Harmony of Tone Masses.—The rhythm and harmony of the tones also assist the composition. As the top of the cube, Fig. 19, is the light-

est tint, the left side is the next in value, then comes the foreground tone, the shaded side of the cube, the dark tone of the upper background, and finally the darkest tone shown in the cast shadow. If the darker tone had been used in the foreground, and the lighter tone in the background, rhythm would have been destroyed. It must always be borne in mind that tone values are used not only to secure proper concentration of interest and to maintain balance, but also by skilful arrangements of gradations to express rhythm and harmony.

30. Examples of Tone Masses in a Landscape.—In Fig. 20 is shown a clear and easily understood example of balance of tone values. The black or deep gray in the tall tree at the left of the center of the picture balances the mass of white and gray at the right and bottom of the picture, and therefore good composition results. The composition is made still more pleasing because rhythm of values is well shown, the values grading in a curve from the white of the tower down the right side and bottom of picture through the gray of the lower foliage, and up again to the black of the tall tree.

If the tall tree were to be moved to the right of the tower, a certain amount of balance could be maintained but the rhythm of values would be disturbed, and the effect would not be as pleasing as the present arrangement.

31. Use of Tone Masses in Legitimate Illustrations. However simple in arrangement and rendering the typical illustration may appear, the artist always gives consideration to the proper arrangement of the masses of light, shade, and shadow to assist the composition and make the picture illustrate most graphically the quoted passage. A careful inspection of the illustrations in the better magazines will reveal the application by the artist of the principles of tone composition herein discussed.

For example, in the illustration shown in the frontispiece, facing page 1 of the text, good composition has been secured not only by means of the simple expedient of having all the men in the picture looking toward the papers spread out on the desk, but also by means of the very light value, almost a brilliant tone,

of the table and the papers.   This light tone is sharply contrasted with the deep values on the clothing of the man with his
back to the observer and on the coat of the man at his right,
and also with the dark gray and black seen at the lower right-
hand corner of the picture.   This sharp contrast is then relieved
by the medium values on the walls, the window shade, and the
clothing of some of the men at the rear of the group.   Note
should also be taken of
the bright lights (high-
lights) on the chair,
the bookcase, the
men's clothing, etc.

Fig. 21

**32.   Use of Bold,
Sharply Contrasted
Values.**—In Fig. 21,
the practical applica-
tion of the principles of
composition is shown
in a bold graphic man-
ner.   The boy seated
on the stone is Dick
Whittington looking
at the distant city of
London, a situation
from the old story
familiar to every one.
It is evident that it
was necessary here to
show two features of
interest, the hero of the tale, Dick Whittington, and the distant
city of London.   The artist has cleverly done this by making the
boy large and placing him prominently in the lower left-hand part
of the picture, portraying him with white masses and in outline.
The large solid-black portions of the upper part of the picture
serve as a setting for and also throw into prominence the figure
of the boy.   This principle of well-arranged, and well-contrasted,
areas of white and of black results in effective compositions.

As a second feature of importance, the distant city is delight-
fully suggested in the upper right-hand corner by a few simple
lines.   It is brought into particular prominence by the broad

By permission of Macmillan and Company, Limited, London

FIG. 22

belt of black foliage at the right middle portion of the picture,
which separates the trees and distant city from the road in
the foreground.   If this black mass were taken away, the
effect of two features of interest would be marred and the entire
composition spoiled.

33. Balance is very effectively shown in this composition. The combined blacks in the upper part of the picture balance the large mass of white in the lower part; and the masses of black, gray, and white on the left side balance the masses of gray, black, and white on the right side. The large black mass of the tree in the upper left-hand corner is broken by introducing the decorative white shield on which is very appropriately emblazoned in half-silhouette the cat, Dick Whittington's companion in his days of poverty. This simple black-and-white drawing will graphically teach more about correct composition and effective concentration of interest than would many pretentious paintings.

34. Use of Small Mass of Dark for Balance.—Fig. 22 shows an interesting application of the principle of a small mass of black balancing a large mass of light or gray. The Gothic structure in the center of the picture would in itself be interesting but monotonous. The introduction of the figures of the woman and the boy in the lower right-hand corner introduce contrast, and as a black mass, serve to balance the large gray mass of the central portion of the picture. The importance of these two figures can be seen by covering them and noting how weak is the picture without them.

35. Methods of Concentrating Interest.—It has been shown that the chief effort in pictorial composition should be to concentrate the interest of the observer upon some particular part or parts so that they may tell the story with greatest effectiveness. Interest may be concentrated by any one of a number of ways.

If the picture contains a series of lines all pointing to, or converging toward, the chief object of interest, like the converging lines of a spider web, the eye will naturally follow these lines to their point of meeting and thus come to the object or figure to be emphasized.

36. Another method is to introduce into the picture something, as a doorway, that will serve as a frame, and place within this whatever is to be emphasized. The eye will naturally

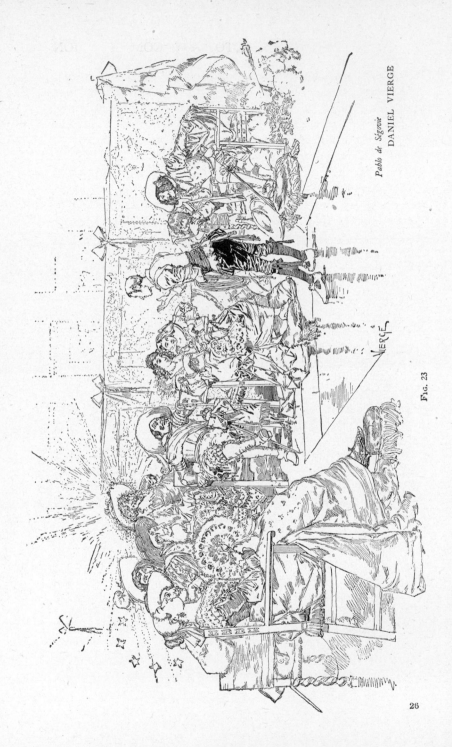

Pablo de Ségovie DANIEL VIERGE

Fig. 23

26

be focused on that which is placed within the frame. This is illustrated in many pictures where it is seen that the interest is centered in the figure of a person entering a doorway.

37. One of the most effective ways, however, of concentrating interest is to arrange the picture so that nearly every one in the picture is looking at or toward the person or object to be emphasized.

FIG. 24

This principle is illustrated in Fig. 23, a reproduction of one of Daniel Vierge's masterful pen drawings, in which no doubt is left that the interest of every one is centered in the figure standing slightly to the right of the center of the picture, who is telling the story. Assistance is given to this concentration of interest by the use of black on the clothing of the story teller, whereas the costumes of his listeners are rendered largely in outline or light grays.

38. In Fig. 24, a reproduction of a modern magazine illustration, every one at the right and the center of the picture has his interest concentrated in the story teller at the extreme left of the picture. They are all looking toward him, which causes the observer of the picture to do likewise, thus concentrating interest on him.

39. Importance of Color in Composition.—The consideration of composition in this subject will be confined to lines, outlined spaces, and black, gray, and white-toned masses. It must not be forgotten, however, that the skilful use of color will serve to center the interest or to preserve the emphasis of a prominent figure. For instance, in a picture of Revolutionary times, attention may be called to a particular British soldier or officer by placing him somewhat in the foreground and making his uniform a pure warm red, whereas the red uniforms of the other soldiers are grayed and thus kept down in prominence or intensity. Similarly, a red handkerchief knotted about the neck of an individual in a picture may center the interest in that particular figure. Vice versa, the prominent figure may be one portrayed in quiet colors amidst a surrounding of brilliant colors.

40. Making Small-Scale Preliminary Sketches.—The next step is to make several (as many as six or eight) little sketches to show various arrangements, as to line and mass, for placing the principal and the subordinate figures in the illustration. Each of these little sketches should be quite small, say 1 in. × 1½ in., or even less, but should be of exactly the same proportions as the large drawing. For instance, if the large drawing is 10 in. × 15 in. the small sketch may be 1 in. × 1½ in., for then each dimension will be exactly one-tenth of the corresponding ones on the large sketch. These little sketches, however, should be simply diagrams roughly blocked in to show proper arrangements of masses in accordance with the principles of composition already learned.

(a)

(b)

(c)

(d)

(e)

(f)

(g)

(h)

F_IG. 25

41. Let it be supposed that the following passage from a story is to be illustrated: "When busily engaged at his desk, Holden was disturbed by Wells throwing open the office door and rushing into the room, holding a newspaper in his outstretched hand."

Assuming that Holden is the most important feature, he may be placed to one side of the center line and very prominent in the foreground; Wells, and his newspaper, may then be placed to the other side of the center line and very prominent in the background; such a trial arrangement is shown in Fig. 25 (a). Or, as another trial arrangement, as shown in (b), Holden may be given still greater prominence by placing him nearer in the foreground and increasing his size by showing only his head, back, right arm, and part of his desk.

In sketch (c), Holden is made the prominent feature by giving a full-face view of him seated at his desk, which is placed in the center of the picture, while only a part of Wells is shown.

In (d) and (e) are shown other small trial sketches that might be made, with the greatest dimension horizontally; and in (f), (g), and (h), other vertical sketches trying out various arrangements of the two figures, the open door, and the desk accessories. It will be seen that these small sketches, which simply show arrangement and are not in any respect detailed, are all correctly arranged according to unity, balance, rhythm, harmony, concentration of interest, etc. In any such series there must always be one that is more pleasing and more suitable than any other. Let it be considered in this case that the most pleasing arrangement is sketch (b). The reason for choosing (b) may be wholly aside from any considerations of superior composition; it may be felt, perhaps, that in sketch (b) there are greater possibilities of securing action, proper expressions, suitable accessories, etc., when this sketch is worked up.

42. Blocking In and Completing the Full-Size Drawing.—It is the purpose here to show how the various elements or details are put together, so as to make a picture, rather than to show how to render a full-size drawing for some definite purpose. It therefore supplements the training in portraying

Fig. 26

objects and scenes in their proper perspective proportions and relations.

As preliminary practice, let it be assumed that the thumb-nail sketch shown in Fig. 25 (*b*) is selected as the one to draw and render full size for a fiction illustration. If it is made on illustrators' board, the trouble of stretching water-color paper on the drawing board is avoided. After the desired size of the picture is laid out on the illustrators' board, the room details are laid out in parallel perspective. This perspective is used because the only vanishing lines are those of a small section of the room interior. Next Holden and the desk are placed in the immediate foreground, Holden being placed to the left of the center line. Wells, and the doorway through which he enters, may then be placed at the upper right.

43. The desk should be drawn in its proper scaled relation to the rest of the room, from a knowledge of actual measure-ments, and with its top and all the desk accessories thereon vanishing in proper parallel perspective. The chair should then be drawn with similar care as to proportion and contour lines. Then draw Holden seated in the chair and looking toward the door, the horizon, or eyelevel, line passing through the level of his eyes. Next, the doorway and the door itself in their proper proportions should be drawn, and the figure of Wells sketched in the doorway, with eyes at the proper pre-determined level, and the head and figure arranged in proper relation to the doorway. This blocks in the main part of the picture. The subordinate details, such as picture and calendar on the wall, desk accessories, etc., may then be drawn in to fill the vacant spaces. It is understood that all this draw-ing is done in pencil, and every object and figure very thoroughly modeled, all rules and principles of drawing and rendering as learned so far being applied to the making of the drawing.

44. In rendering the drawing in wash, gouache, or whatever medium is used, the artist must have planned out first of all what tones are to be used. The principles of properly portray-ing good composition and concentration of interest by means of tone values must be carefully considered, and then the actual rendering must be made to carry out the proper laws of tone value composition. It is not required that the details of such rendering should be discussed here, for full training in such rendering work is given elsewhere. The final rendering will appear as in Fig. 26.

EXAMPLES OF COMPOSITION IN PICTORIAL WORK

SINGLE-FIGURE COMPOSITION

45. It has been the purpose of this subject to give a comprehensive explanation of the principles of pictorial composition. The application of these principles is best shown by the study of the compositions of well-known artists. For this reason, there are reproduced here a number of composition illustrations by well-known artists, which are analyzed and the methods by which the artist secured his results are pointed out.

From the standpoint of composition, these illustrations naturally divide themselves into several distinct classes, as follows: (1) Illustrations in which the interest is confined to a single figure, whether that figure is in solitude or in a crowd; (2) illustrations in which the interest is divided between two figures, one of chief importance and the other of secondary importance; (3) illustrations where three or more figures are used; and (4) illustrations where a large group or crowd occupies the allotted space, the interest being divided in various ways in different conditions.

46. Illustrations With Isolated Figure.—In preparing an illustration with a single figure that is quite large, the general contour or silhouette of the figure must fit well into the space or outline it is to occupy, so that no awkward vacant spaces result. Thus, an erect full-length figure fits most appropriately into a tall, narrow, rectangular space; a front-view seated figure into a shorter rectangular space; and profile seated figure into a square. The erect figure will not look well in the square, nor will the seated figure in profile look well in the tall narrow rectangle. In case the single figure does not nearly fill the

allotted space, there is not such necessity for planning it to fill
the contours or outlines of the space as when it entirely occupies
the space.

In modern book and magazine illustration, the demands of
page size, column size, etc., are such as to make the majority
of illustrations of a somewhat arbitrary rectangular shape,
somewhat higher than wide. As a result, the modern illustrator, when using a single figure, makes it comparatively small and
well placed near the center of the rectangular outline, filling the
surrounding space with pictorial accessories of a suitable nature.

47. In Fig. 27 is shown an example of the single figure, with
no animate surroundings whatever. Here the interest is centered entirely upon the young man seated at the tool bench,
looking at the blueprint. This picture illustrates a story that
tells about a young man, while temporarily employed in a
carpenter shop, seeing a blueprint for the first time and thus
learning of the profession of architecture. It is well worth
studying for many reasons. In the first place, the illustrator
selected an important incident to portray the young man's
intense interest in a blueprint, which incident foreshadowed
the climax of the story; namely, his becoming a successful architect. Then, too, the proper surroundings are expressed. The
man is not shown studying, or working upon a blueprint on an
architect's drawing table, but is shown intently and curiously
looking at a blueprint spread out on the carpenter's work
bench. There are the bench, vise, the steel square, the plane
and the shavings, the glue pot, etc., everything according
exactly with the text of the story. The young man is shown
coatless and with sleeves rolled up, and his face well expressing
puzzled interest. The beginner should take a lesson from this,
which lesson is that all details and accessories of the picture
should be consistent, and should exactly accord with the text
of the story.

48. The perspective and composition are well thought out
and expressed in the illustration in Fig. 27. The eye level of
the man marks the horizon; all details below it, as window sash,
edges of tool bench, box, etc., vanish upwards, left and right,

Fig. 27

FIG. 28

36

and all details above his eye level vanish downwards left and right, the whole being undoubtedly in 45° perspective. The placing of the eager interested face of the man near the center of the picture, and having it thrust forwards, concentrates

FIG. 29

interest thereon, which is assisted by the main lines of the picture leading toward, and pointing to, the man as he is seated at the end of the carpenter's bench. The proper arrangements of the tone values in the rendering also assist in making this an effective composition illustration.

49. In Fig. 28 is shown another example of an illustration with a single isolated figure. This illustration is made by the same artist that painted the one in Fig. 27. The composition here is in the inverted pyramid form, the wainscoting forming the top of the inverted pyramid and the front corner of the rug being the apex of the pyramid. Thus the figure of the man intently reading the letter is brought into prominence at once; and the desk and room accessories, although clearly shown, do not detract from this prominence. The method of rendering, with clear-cut, crisp, brush strokes showing, should be carefully noted.

50. Still another example of the single isolated figure is shown in Fig. 29, which needs few explanatory remarks. This shows the workman at the noon lunch hour improving his spare time by study while he lunches. Not only is the interest well centered on the workman, but the artist has painstakingly and accurately portrayed, by the character of the machinery, that the workman is employed in a machine shop, which helps to carry out and conform with the text of the story that is illustrated.

51. Illustrations With Single Figure Detached From Others.—Situations will constantly arise in commercial advertisement illustrating, newspaper illustrating, cartooning, and fiction illustrating where the interest must be concentrated or focused on one character and what he is doing, although there are other characters introduced into the picture to bring out the action and to tell the story of the incident portrayed. Such an illustration is shown in Fig. 30. The story tells of a young man, out of a position temporarily but not yet in the down-and-out class, who has just had an interview with a man who has refused to give him a position. The picture portrays the young man going out of the building into a driving snowstorm, which helps to add hopelessness to that he already feels.

The custodian standing in the vestibule shows that it is an office or bank building and that the young man is not a thief but a visitor to the building, and that his appearance of dejection and hopelessness are so unusual as to cause interest, and

39 Fig. 30

perhaps comment, from an individual as used to odd sights of all kinds as is the custodian of a public building.

Fig. 31

The sharp contrasts of dark and light, and the brilliant lighting of the man's face against a dark background, help in accomplishing the graphic portrayal of this incident of the story.   In this case, also, the clear-cut, crisp brush stroke work should be noticed.

52. In Fig. 31 is reproduced another illustration in which the interest is centered upon the man in the foreground, but assisted by other persons in the picture (or suggested by the picture). The man with the revolver has been made to hold the most prominent place by making him the largest figure in the picture, and placing him near its center; also by making his clothes dark in contrast to a brilliantly lighted fence and foreground, which looks as if a searchlight were thrown upon it. The fact that he is being pursued, and probably shot at, by his enemies is clearly shown by his turning around in his flight and shooting as he turned. The man inside the fence, shotgun in hand, is ready to protect himself and family from the pursuer or the pursued should it be necessary. This illustration is an excellent one for the study of action, methods of rendering, the balancing of light against dark, and many other methods of securing good composition that have been described in this subject.

_____

TWO-FIGURE COMPOSITION

53. Illustrations Showing Attraction.—The very fact that there are two figures in a picture presupposes that they have some relation to each other and therefore that they will be placed so near to each other as to form a single mass or unit in the composition. This single mass, in the case of a two-figure illustration, may generally be considered as being included in a vertical ellipse or a horizontal ellipse, most likely the former because the average page illustration in a magazine or book is a vertical rectangle.

Various methods are employed to show that the two figures in the composition are connected in interest. The two figures may be looking directly at each other or at some common object near them or they may be touching each other, as with outstretched arm, etc. The eye then naturally jumps from one to the other and thus the interest is properly distributed, which is what the artist intended to do. It is not always possible to convey by the picture itself the idea as to which figure in a two-figure composition is of the most importance. This must be told most frequently by the context of the story.

43   Fig. 33

54. In Figs. 32, 33, 34, and 35 are shown examples of two-figure compositions.   In some cases, unity or sameness of interests is shown, while in other cases there is separation or antagonism.   These elements of unity or antagonism need not be physical; they may be expressed by the attitudes, the facial expressions, and so on, of the two individuals in the picture. To arrange with proper story-telling effect, the two figures in a composition requires a keen study of the passage to be illustrated, and a careful analysis must be made as to which person in the picture must be given prominence, and which one is to be kept subordinate, and just how this is to be done.   As will be revealed from the comments made on the illustrations in Figs. 32, 33, 34, and 35, there will be need for good arrangement from the standpoint of drawing, but also careful arrangement of tone values—lights, shades, and shadows.   Not only should the illustrations be studied to get these principles, but careful observations and study of illustrations in current magazines should be made.

55. In Fig. 32, the interest of the invalid mother in her son's worries is clearly shown by the manner in which her arm and hand are placed upon the shoulder of the young man.   The elliptic composition is clearly shown here, the ellipse containing the two figures being placed somewhat to the left in the picture. In the illustration, a common interest is manifest by the manner in which the old lady looks at her son.

56. In Fig. 33 the community of interest, or fellow feeling, is shown by the fact that both mother and daughter are sewing at home by lamplight.   Further, the proximity of the two figures, the manner in which the garments upon which they are working blend, and the lines leading from one to the other, all assist to establish unity of interest.   Points in the rendering that assist the composition and that should be noted are: The silhouetting of the blond-haired girl with light waist against a dark background; the contrast of the black dress of the mother with the white garment upon which she is sewing; the relieving of the black background by the framed picture with its high lights; and the very graphic manner in which the effect of the lamplight has been shown.

57. Sometimes such an effect is secured by placing both persons on the same divan or couch, the leaning forward of one toward the other in a half-playful manner, and a comfortable, self-satisfied, smiling attitude of both, may express an interest in common, even though the two figures are not actually close together. The whole effect may be heightened by dispensing with practically all the background.

58. Illustrations Showing Antagonism.—The illustrator of fiction is called upon to illustrate situations in many cases where there is antagonism or diversity of interest. By antagonism, however, is not meant actual physical encounter, where one man shoots another or knocks him down with a blow of the fist; such antagonism can very easily be portrayed. But circumstances must at times be illustrated where the two figures in the composition are not in exact accord, not in harmonious relationship. Examples of such two-figure illustrations are shown in Figs. 34 and 35. In each case it will be observed that the feeling of antagonism is expressed in part by placing between the two figures some object that serves as a physical barrier, such as a desk, a table, a counter, or other object.

59. One well-known illustration of this kind, not reproduced in this text, showed a young man being told, by an older one, that his services would not be needed. The elder man, seated back of a massive desk, was dignified and courteous in bearing, but no doubt was left in the reader's mind that his very bearing and dignity, and the massive desk that separated him from the young man, portrayed the separation, or even latent antagonism that exists in such situations. In order to portray the situation most forcibly, very little background, or even desk details, were emphasized, so that the reader's interest would be concentrated on the two contrasted figures and their expressions.

60. In Fig. 34, this feeling of separation is expressed by the small desk at which is seated the man smoking the cigar.

Whether or not there is any pronounced antagonism between
the two persons in the picture, it is very evident which is the
"boss."   Attention is again called to the correct perspective

Fig. 34

of this picture, the lines of the mullions of the window, and those
of the desk and its details, etc., vanishing properly.   The position of the eye-level line is very evident.   The skilful manner
in which the lights and darks have been used should not be lost
sight of, for by them have been portrayed balance and harmony
of values.

61. The separation of interests and of types between the alert experienced traveling man leaning on the counter and the lazy clerk back of the counter is well shown in Fig. 35. Acute antagonism is avoided, and an effort to equalize differences in type is made by showing the traveling man leaning pleasantly

FIG. 35

and familiarly on the counter. No artist who was not well trained in perspective could have drawn the counter, show cases, and other details of the store fixtures, as they are drawn.

62. An illustration such as this should convince the beginner that much study and observation as to local color and details are necessary before even the simple blocking out of the skeleton plan for the illustration is done. The experienced

I L T 22—13

illustrator takes his sketch pad to local scenes (as a store interior, in this case) and makes faithful and realistic studies of such interiors and scenes, and does not make the error of relying on his memory or imagination.

THREE- OR FOUR-FIGURE COMPOSITIONS

63. The underlying principles of space filling referred to in the case of one-figure and two-figure illustrations, apply also

Fig. 36

in the case of illustrations with three or four figures. Various geometrical shapes, as the ellipse, rectangle, triangle, etc., may be employed as the underlying forms of the compositions.

It must be understood, of course, that the geometrical or basic character of such foundation shapes must not be too evident, but they must be there nevertheless. The reason for this is that the eye of the reader or observer is most accustomed to the observation of simple shapes, either in three dimensions or

Fig. 37

only in two.   When, therefore, the illustrator bases his pictures on certain well-known shapes (as the triangle, the square, the circle, etc.), the observer feels more comfortable when looking at such a picture, and the illustration is therefore successful in composition.

64.   In Fig. 36 is shown a typical three-figure composition— three members of the family reading and studying by the evening lamp.   Points to note well are the clever arrangement of the lamp so that its direct light does not shine into the eyes of the observer but is partly eclipsed by the profile of the mother's head in the foreground and the light shining on to the faces of the son and the daughter in the back of the picture.   The portrayal of black darkness outside the window heightens the effect of its being a night scene.   The balance and harmony of values in this composition are excellent, and the young artist should study it with great care.

65.   In Fig. 37 is reproduced an illustration in which the two men in the foreground are important.   On whom the interest is concentrated, while the women in the distance are not particularly important, but are needed because called for by the story.   Here the most prominent figure in the story is placed in the vertical center of the picture, while the caller, being of secondary interest, is placed to one side.   The student will have learned already to recognize how this picture was planned from the standpoints of perspective and composition.   It is only necessary, therefore, to call attention to the very simple attitude of the older man.   As his coat is off and a pipe is in one hand while with the other he carries a chair for the visitor, this attitude tells graphically that he was resting after his evening meal when the door bell rang and he welcomed the visitor. The dignity and bearing of the caller show clearly that his mission is a friendly one.   The very human curiosity of the women in the kitchen is admirably portrayed.

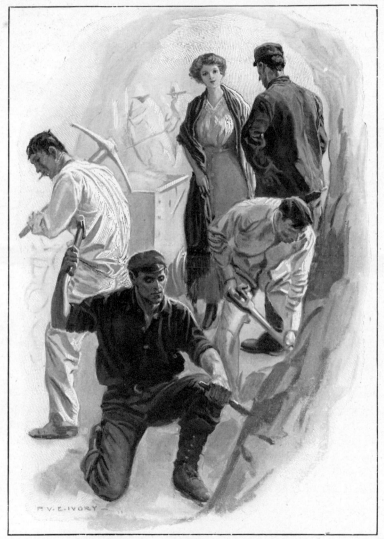

Fig. 38

GROUPS AND CROWDS IN COMPOSITIONS

66. When an illustration contains over four or five persons or figures of importance it may be considered as coming under the group or crowd class. To portray a crowd of persons in an illustration requires considerable skill. Not only must the principal figures be given the proper degree of prominence, but the minor figures must be relatively placed. As the number of figures in the picture increases, the difficulties of correct composition and rendering increase.

67. Excellent composition, from the standpoint of balance, harmony, and contrast of tone values, is shown in the illustration reproduced in Fig. 38. The dark clothes of the miner in the foreground chiseling into the rock are silhouetted against the white and the light gray clothes of the other workmen. For that reason the size and blackness of value of the figure in the foreground do not make it the most important figure in the composition. These details lead the eye of the observer upward and backward to the figures of the girl and the man at the top of the picture, who are themselves silhouetted against the white background and are the important figures in the composition.

68. In Fig. 39 is reproduced an illustration that shows very graphically a crowd in action. The composition is clearly based on the inverted pyramid. The disheveled figure that is being chased occupies the foreground and all the pursuers are portrayed as running toward the observer. While the action, in this case the various portrayals of the action of running, is the important thing, it is interesting to note the different tone values with which the clothes of the various pursuing figures are painted, thus giving snap and sparkle to them, and avoiding monotony of tone values.

69. It is not particularly difficult for the artist to arrange a good composition in which the figures, animals, etc., are in repose, or at rest. However, when very violent action is being portrayed, as in the group of running men in Fig. 39, not only is a thorough training in drawing the figure in action necessary, but the laws of good composition must take account of the necessity of suggesting to the reader that the running figures are moving rapidly and that the proportions of composition plan may suddenly change. In such a situation the illustrator relies on the use of the triangular shape to serve as a basic structure of his picture, because the triangular shape is flexible, and may "stretch," and still retain the basic features of a triangle.

FIG. 39

70. The illustration shown in the frontispiece, facing page 1, is an example of a fully and completely rendered illustration. Not only are all the figures placed and rendered to bring out most clearly the story of a board of directors examining some plans prepared by the young man on the left, but the furniture, walls, window, window shade, pictures on walls, chandelier, etc., have been rendered with clearness and precision. The render-

Drawn by I.C.S. Student C. M. Dugger, Jr.
Retained by Permission.

FIG. 40

Drawn by I.C.S. Student C. M. Dugger, Jr.
Retained by Permission.

FIG. 41

ing, on all four sides of the picture, has been carried out to the edges of the picture and is finished off squarely against the white paper, and added snap is secured by the use of the black line surrounding the picture.

The entire setting for the scene was first laid out in angular perspective, then all details of walls, window, door, furniture, etc., were correctly drawn in perspective. The principal figures on the right are silhouetted against the white window, and the young man, who is the hero of the story, is given prominence by isolating him at the left of the picture and yet really including him in the group. This is a well-plotted, well-composed, excellently rendered, and in every way a thoroughly finished, illustration and deserves particularly careful study.

71. Example of Student's Original Composition. Reference has been made earlier in this subject to the manner in which the illustrator is accustomed to prepare what are known as thumbnail sketches of proportioned arrangements of the figures and of landscape accessories for the illustrating of the particular passage that has been quoted. In Fig. 40 are shown four thumbnail sketches, and in Fig. 41 a large completed drawing, of pictorial arrangements to illustrate the following quoted passage: "Willie, her ten-year-old son, was just leaving the house on an errand; the mother watching him from the open doorway." This work was done by a student of this particular subject and well illustrates just how even the beginner works when blocking in thumbnail sketches and making large drawings.

It will be observed that, after having made, and then carefully considered, the sketches made for Fig. 40, the student decided that he wanted to use the fourth one, believing that this one would work out better than any of the others. He might have used the first one, or the third one, because either one of these would have worked up well. However, he doubtless selected the fourth one because the boy is portrayed in a rather unusual manner. In the fourth sketch, and in the large drawing for Fig. 41, the boy appears to possess a very apparent disinclination to go on the errand, thus adding a humorous touch.

These two illustrations are introduced here, not only to show progress by the one who studies this subject, but also to illustrate the method of laying out the preliminary sketches, selecting the desired one, and then working it up full size. The original rendering for Fig. 41 was done in delicate washes of water color, and therefore it was possible for the student to portray the effect of sunlight shining onto the porch floor and, of the shadow cast by the porch roof and the pediment. The shadow of the boy as it falls on the porch floor is particularly good, not only in its shape but in its semitransparency. In fact, the semitransparent quality of the shadows in the rendering is evident throughout all the shadows.

It is the posture and action of each figure, however, that should be most carefully observed. Anyone working out a problem such as this will profit by a careful examination of Figs. 40 and 41. It is understood, of course, that no one of these sketches is to be copied when any of the required work on the plates in this subject is prepared. The student must use original arrangements and make original drawings.

PICTORIAL COMPOSITION EXERCISES

GENERAL INFORMATION

72. Required Work in Pictorial Composition.—While much can be learned from precept and example in the study of composition, the only sure way of knowing whether the instructions are properly understood, and can be applied to practical work, is to prepare composition drawings. To serve as such a test is the purpose of the work required in this subject.

The work required consists of exercises arranged as three drawing plates, each 10 in. $\times$ 15 in., or one-half of the regular 15"$\times$20" sheet of cold-pressed (white) drawing paper, or of Whatman's cold-pressed water-color paper. As before, the plates are to be sent to the Schools for inspection in the order specified, and while the plates received are being examined and returned the student will be working on the special work required on the following plates.

73. Preliminary Practice Work (NOT To Be Sent In).—Although Plate 1 of this subject may really be considered as preliminary or elementary arrangements of objects and groupings for pictorial composition work, yet, before Plate 2 and those that follow are attempted, further preliminary practice work should be done as described in the succeeding paragraphs. This work is NOT to be sent in to the Schools; only regular plates are to be submitted.

The first practice work is to be done on a sheet of white paper of the usual size arranged vertically; that is, 10 inches wide by 15 inches high, divided vertically and horizontally, so as to make four subordinate rectangles each 5 inches wide by $7\frac{1}{2}$ inches high. Each exercise will then occupy one rectangle. Using the finder to make a proper selection, make four completely rendered pencil drawings, direct from nature. A $\frac{1}{2}$-inch white margin should show around each drawing. These sketches should conform in all respects to the principles of pictorial perspective and pictorial composition. They may portray four different subjects, or four different views or arrangements of the same subject. Among the subjects that may be used are: A house or group of houses flanked by trees, standing on a street or road; a view of a distant town indicating the buildings, as seen across fields from a hill or mountain; a view in a city or town street, showing buildings, vehicles, people, etc.

A similar sheet should be arranged vertically; that is, 10 inches wide by 15 inches high. Then, select from the four nature composition sketches drawn for Plate 2 the one that appears to be most nearly correct in composition and, therefore, most pleasing. Draw and render this one in soft pencil to an enlarged scale, allowing a margin of about $1\frac{1}{2}$ inches or more all around the drawing, thus making the drawing itself about 7 inches wide by 10 inches or 12 inches high. (If desired, a totally different view, drawn direct from nature, may be substituted.) This sketch should be worked up with the greatest care and degree of finish, so that all lines, masses, and tone values occupy their proper places in a well-balanced and harmonious composition.

As previously advised, none of this preliminary practice work should be sent in to the Schools. Only the regular plates, with definite numbers, as described in the following articles, should be submitted.

PLATE 1

74. Special Directions for Plate 1.—The four composition drawings on this sheet, Plate 1, must be carefully planned and drawn in accordance with the principles of composition, as already explained. No haphazard sketches of these models, or any sketches made roughly without thought of proper composition, or copied from any text illustrations, will be accepted.

75. Exercise A, Plate 1.—Plate 1 is to be arranged vertically; that is, 10 inches wide by 15 inches high, and divided vertically and horizontally so as to make four subordinate rectangles each 5 inches wide by $7\frac{1}{2}$ inches high.

Exercise A, is to occupy the upper left-hand $5'' \times 7\frac{1}{2}''$ rectangle. Using the cardboard frame or finder to make a proper selection, make a completely rendered pencil drawing of the wooden model of the cube seen at an angle and conventionally lighted so as to cast its shadow toward the right, thus expressing proper composition. Consider not only the mass of the cube itself, but also the cast shadow, the table line, the shapes of background spaces, and the relative tone values of foreground and background space. Show a $\frac{1}{2}$-inch margin of white paper all around the drawing.

76. Exercise B, Plate 1.—Exercise B is to occupy the upper right-hand $5'' \times 7\frac{1}{2}''$ rectangle. Using the finder to make a proper selection, make a completely rendered pencil drawing of the wooden model of the pyramid seen at an angle and conventionally lighted, so as to cast its shadow toward the right, thus expressing proper composition. Consider not only the mass of the pyramid itself but also the cast shadow, the table line, the shape of the background spaces, and the relative tone values of foreground and background spaces. Show a ½-inch margin of white paper all around the drawing.

77. Exercise C, Plate 1.—Exercise C is to occupy the lower left-hand 5″×7½″ rectangle. Using the finder to make a proper selection, make a completely rendered pencil drawing of the wooden models of the pyramid and cube properly grouped in correct composition, unity, balance, rhythm, and harmony being properly shown. Consider not only the proper arrangement of the two objects in relation to each other and to the outline of the enclosing rectangle, but also the shapes of the background spaces and the relative tone values of the composition. Show a ½-inch margin of white paper all around the drawing.

78. Exercise D, Plate 1.—Exercise D is to occupy the lower right-hand 5″×7½″ rectangle. Using the finder to make a proper selection, make a completely rendered pencil drawing of the wooden models of the cone, the cube, and the sphere properly grouped in correct composition. Consider not only the proper arrangement of the objects in relation to one another and to the outline of the enclosing rectangle, but also the shapes of the background spaces and the relative tone values of the composition. Show a ½-inch margin of white paper all around the drawing.

79. Final Work on Plate 1.—Letter or write the title, Plate 1: Pictorial Composition, at the top of the sheet just completed, and on the lower left-hand corner of the back place class letters and number, name, address, and the date of completing the plate. Roll the plate, place it in the mailing tube, and send to the Schools for inspection. Then proceed with Plate 2.

PLATE 2

80. Exercises A, B, C, and D, Plate 2.—Plate 2 is to be arranged vertically; that is, 10 inches wide by 15 inches high. To draw it, prepare four preliminary sketches for a composition illustration for the following quoted passage:

"Willie, her 10-year-old son, was just leaving the house on an errand; the mother watching him from the open doorway." These preliminary sketches should be at least 2 in.×3½ in., and the four grouped near the center of the sheet. They should be carefully prepared after the method illustrated in Fig. 25 and described in the accompanying text. No effort should be made to work up the rendering in detail, but all tone values should be indicated by broad masses made with pencil strokes, Great care should be observed in applying all the principles of pictorial perspective and pictorial composition. None of this work is to be hastily dashed off, but the arrangement of each composition sketch must be thought out very carefully, and then drawn in mass so that each sketch is a clear plan of a proposed picture. Draw the mother and her boy from living models.

The successful working out of this composition sketch will require an intelligent application of all the drawing and composition training so far given, and should be further prepared for by a study of similar pictures in current magazines and books.

81. Final Work on Plate 2.—Letter or write the title, Plate 2: Pictorial Composition, at the top of the sheet just completed, and on the lower left-hand corner of the back place class letters and number, name, address, and the date of completing the plate. Lay the plate aside until Plate 3 is completed, at which time Plates 2 and 3 can be sent to the Schools together for inspection. Proceed now with Plate 3.

PLATE 3

82. Preliminary Blocking-in for Plate 3.—Plate 3 is to be arranged vertically; that is, 10 inches wide by 15 inches high. To draw it, select from the four preliminary sketches drawn for Plate 2 the one that appears to be most nearly correct in composition and, therefore, most pleasing. Draw and render in soft pencil, in broad masses—not in finished detail—this one to an enlarged scale, allowing a margin of about 1½ inches, or more, all around the drawing, thus making the drawing itself about 7 inches wide by 10 inches or 12 inches high. This sketch is not to be the final, detailed, rendering of this picture, but is to be simply the full-size blocking in of the lines and masses of the picture, being done with bold but carefully placed strokes of the pencil, and all tones being given their proper values. In other words, the sketch is to serve as a full-size preliminary, or foundation, drawing on which the final rendering is to be based.

83. **Finished Rendering for Plate 3.**—Now, using this blocked-in pencil drawing as a foundation sketch, prepare a finished, detailed rendering of this composition illustration, about 7 inches wide by 10 inches or 12 inches high, rendering it in charcoal (fixed), pen and ink, wash, gouache, or water color, as desired. The student is advised to do his very best in the drawing, the composition, and the rendering of this illustration—for it will be of practical value to him as a training for future work. Use living models for the figures.

84. **Final Work on Plate 3.**—Letter or write the title, Plate 3: Pictorial Composition, at the top of the sheet just completed, and on the lower left-hand corner of the back place class letters and number, name, address, and the date of completing the plate, and send the plate to the Schools for inspection. Whether or not the plate may be rolled or be sent flat must be influenced by the manner in which it is rendered and the character of the paper or board. If rendered in charcoal or pen and ink on Whatman's, Strathmore, or linen ledger paper, it may be rolled as before and sent in a tube. If rendered on heavy bristol board or on Steinbach or illustrators' board, which cannot be rolled, it must be packed flat and mailed in that form for examination.

If any redrawn or rerendered work on any of the plates of this subject has been called for and has not yet been completed, it should be satisfactorily finished at this time. After all required work on the plates has been completed the work of the next subject should be taken up at once.